Four-Engined

co 4A

Boulton and Paul

Brit

Vickers "Vimy"

B.A.T. "Bantam"

uport (Fr.)

Caudron Twin-Engine Passenger Type (Fr.)

S.P.A.D. (Fr.

Three-Engined Caproni Biplane (Ital.)

Gotha Bomber (Ger.)

Friedrichshafen Bomber (Ger.)

OVER THERE IN THE AIR

C. A. Brannen Series
Texas A&M University Press
College Station

OVER THERE IN THE AIR

The Fightin' Texas Aggies
in World War I,
1917–1918

JOHN A. ADAMS JR. '73

TEXAS A&M UNIVERSITY PRESS
COLLEGE STATION

Library of Congress Control Number: 2019947779
ISBN 13: 978-1-62349-845-0 (cloth: alk. paper)
978-1-62349-846-7 (Ebook)

In Honor of my Granddad,
Pvt. Reps Miller
146th Machine Gun Bn, 41st Division
1918–1919,
and
Ronald Sims Adams

CONTENTS

OVER THERE IN THE AIR

INTRODUCTION

Man is not a farmer, or a professor, or an engineer, but he is all. Man is priest, and scholar, and statesman, and professor, and soldier.

——Ralph W. Emerson, August 31, 1837

In the months following the outbreak of World War I (WWI) in the fall of 1914, numerous Americans, including a cross-section of student cadets and alumni of the Agricultural and Mechanical (A&M) College of Texas —the Texas Aggies—would sail to Europe to volunteer to join foreign armies and the new "aeroplane" squadrons. The motives for the exodus to enlistment varied, from historic family allegiances to a young man's undefined drive for adventure and glory. The A&M College campus, with the full endorsement of its board of directors and faculty, would be transformed into an extensive training camp for army and navy technicians. Once the US Congress formally declared war in April 1917, hundreds of Texas Aggies and college staff enlisted, trained, and shipped to Europe to join the fight "over there."

The Great War, as WWI was commonly known in that era, surprised most Americans, who by and large had little or no interest in events beyond the daily routine of their families and livelihood. Americans by 1910 were recovering from a couple of mild economic depressions even as agricultural production (and prices) reached historic levels and industry across the country grew and diversified. The national attitude improved in part due to the popularity of Major League Baseball and the spread of college football, which captured the enthusiasm and imagination of those wishing to escape the pressures of recent hard times.

America was in a period of change in many regards, but none was more apparent in everyday life than the ongoing industrial advancements that marked the era. At the turn of the twentieth century, a wave of excitement and technological innovation, pushed forward by the optimistic spirit of the budding industrial revolution of the late 1800s, ushered in new inventions and products that reshaped everyday life, industry, and warfare for the balance of the century. Revolutionary inventions and improvements marked one of the most innovative eras in human history. Medical and pharmaceutical breakthroughs increased life expectancies, the growing application of electricity paved the way for technologies such as the radio and telephone, and advances in transportation, including improved high-speed railroad service, new and faster ship designs, and the emergence of the automobile, along with an increase in bridge building across the country and new "high rises" in urban centers, boosted commerce. Still, the innovation that captured the imagination of an entire generation of ordinary American students, inventors, politicians, entrepreneurs, and military men was flight: aviation and the aeroplane.

This is the first work to chronicle the role and contributions of Texas A&M and its students and former students in WWI. While the college became one of the largest US Army and Navy training centers in the nation for technical services, hundreds of former students, alumni, and staff also entered active duty in the US Army, Navy, Coast Guard, and Marine Corps. Following the outbreak of the European war in the fall of 1914, many Aggies went to France, Great Britain, and Italy at their own expense to volunteer for the newly created military air service, including the fledgling Army Air Service, the forerunner of today's modern US Air Force. Their stories, and those of the Aggies who followed after the formal American declaration of war, have largely been lost over time.

More than 2,300 Texas Aggies (in an era when annual enrollment was about 1,000) served in the Great War in a broad cross-section of assignments. (Students were nicknamed Farmers until the 1920s, when that moniker was replaced by Aggies. For purposes of this work, however, they are called Aggies throughout.) To simplify matters, Texas A&M gradually developed a unique means of categorizing students who had graduated and those who enlisted before graduating. All the Aggies chronicled in this book attended the college and, regardless of whether or not they officially graduated, were considered "former students" or "ex-cadets." Thus, while all had been members of the Texas A&M Corps of Cadets and walked the halls of the college, there evolved during the WWI era three designations to more precisely categorize all who attended.

The first designated those enrolled from one to three years, with an "x" for "former or ex-student" associated with their expected year of graduation, such as 'x18. The second, indicating cadets who graduated and received a diploma, used their class designation only, such as '14 (without the "x"). There was one exception to this category, however. Following the United States' declaration of war in April 1917, the Class of 1917 was rushed into military service at an off-campus officer training camp in Leon Springs, Texas. These Aggies technically did not finish their last few months of classes or sit for final exams prior to the regular commencement ceremonies held every June. The Texas A&M Board of Directors, given the unusual circumstances, approved the awarding of diplomas to the Class of '17 despite the shortfall of the last few weeks of class and exams.

As the war progressed and many more students enlisted in the armed services before completing graduation requirements, the A&M board added a third category of special "Honor War Certificates" to recognize the time spent at Texas A&M by any student who answered the "call of his country to enter the military service of the United States to do his part in the war for democracy and freedom." These former cadets routinely used the "x" to denote what would have been their class affiliation. These certificates were discontinued after the November 1918 armistice, after which many veterans returned to complete their degree, keeping the designation of their original class, regardless of their actual graduation year. The cascade of students and former students who volunteered for the new Army Air Service underscores the more than century-old fascination of Texas Aggies with the aeroplane.

Dr. Henry C. Dethloff, professor emeritus of history at Texas A&M and author of numerous works on both space flight and the history of the university, most notably *A Centennial History of Texas A&M University, 1876–1976* (1975), for decades has noted that "Texas Aggies from the earliest beginnings of the era of aviation have had an affinity for and fascination with flight and flying." Dethloff's own interest in flight, much like that of many early dreamers of air travel, probably began at a young age through science fiction novels, including Jules Verne's classic *De La Tierra á la Luna* (*From Earth to the Moon*), published in 1865. Dethloff's flights in his father's 1940 vintage Aeronca airplane no doubt increased his fascination.

In the spirit of Henry Dethloff's identification of generations of early-twentieth-century Aggies who were intrigued by aviation, this work includes a dozen WWI photographs never before published. These photos of aeroplanes of the era were collected by Pvt. James V. "Pinky" Wilson '21 while on duty in Germany in late 1918 and early 1919. While not an aviator, this young Marine's fascination with flying, and his collected photographs, provide the thread by which the story that follows is woven together. I first was made aware of these images in the fall of 1975, when I traveled to Burnet, Texas, to interview Pinky about the origins of the Texas Aggie War Hymn, the school's fight song that he penned as a single verse during WWI under the original title of "Goodbye to Texas University," referring to the college's athletic archrival. Upon returning to campus after the war to complete his degree, the song was "jazzed up," introduced to the cadets, and soon embraced as the A&M College fight song. In recent years, I rediscovered the Wilson WWI aviation photos in the possession of his grandson, Scott Walterscheid '84, and thank him for allowing their inclusion.

A canvass of WWI unit records with after-action reports, alumni newsletters, personal papers, archival collections, and newspapers helped craft this story of one segment of the Texas Aggie WWI experience—Aggies involved in the birth of military aviation. I have attempted to locate and confirm, with the expert assistance of Bill Page '76, some 250 A&M former students involved in WWI aviation, ranging from pilots and observers to mechanics and members of ground crews. As often as possible, I have used the candid descriptions and correspondence of the participants from the war in France. There is no single, centralized database and no record is fully complete, and I acknowledge that I alone am responsible for the scope of this study and for any errors or omissions.

Special thanks are extended to Carl Walker '73, C. C. Taylor '51, Jerry Cooper '63, Jim Woodall '50, Buck Henderson '62, Tom Darling '54, Don Johnson '50, and David Chapman '67. Additionally, Cushing Archives staff Greg Bailey, Anton DuPlessis, Leslie Winter, and Jenny Reibenspies provided timely assistance.

This is the story of how the A&M College of Texas responded to the war "over here" and the air war in Europe "over there" as told through the actions and memoirs of Texas Aggie aviators and their crews, and reflecting their training and experiences, their fears and valor. Scores of these Fightin' Texas Aggies were at the forefront of the aviation era, both in war and in peace.

Figure 1. James V. "Pinky" Wilson '20 was on active duty in France at the time he penned the Aggie War Hymn. He also collected an extensive set of airplane pictures of the war. These were kept in his footlocker and passed down to family members. Courtesy of Cushing Memorial Library & Archives, Texas A&M University.

JAMES VERNON WILSON
Florence, Texas
Animal Husbandry

Age 22; 6th Regiment U. S. Marines '18-'19; Fish Co. E; Sophomore Co. E 1st; Junior Sergeant Co. E 1st; Chairman Arrangement Committee Junior Banquet '17; Capital City Club '15-'20; Glee Club '16-'20; Ross Volunteer; Casual Co. '19-'20.

"PINKY"

This ex-Marine ought to make a good politician for he is still a good mixer although his talents have suffered somewhat on account of Prohibition. And he has a line that will entertain any crowd from pink tea lounge cooties to a bunch of cow punchers. Pinkey's favorite pastime is supplying minors in the best quartette on the campus. He is not only supreme in the above lines but in his academic work he ranks with the best. Pinkey's wildest idea is to have a million-acre ranch in South America stocked with pure-bred Herefords. Personally, we believe sincerely that Wilson will eventually accomplish this unusual feat and make it a big success. We have the utmost confidence that Wilson will do a Man's part in all progressive effort directed for the benefit of this State and Nation.

1

THE ROAD TO WAR

Germany is now making war on us. She has been making war on us for some time, sinking our ships, even our empty ships homeward bound, and killing our citizens. We see what she is trying to do against us in Mexico. We ought to recognize that a state of war exists.

—David F. Houston
Secretary, US Department of Agriculture
White House cabinet meeting, March 20, 1917
President of Texas A&M, 1902–1905

Having failed in time of peace to prepare for war, the United States and the entente allies will pay for this act of folly before the war ends.

—Col. Teddy Roosevelt

The clouds of war that cast tensions across the European continent erupted in armed mobilization and war in August 1914 following the bloody assassination by a Serbian terrorist on a side street in Sarajevo, Bosnia, of Archduke Franz Ferdinand of Austria and his wife, Sophie, on June 28, 1914. This was but the first shot following years of pent-up, Machiavellian maneuvering, jealousies, and frustrations that finally exploded, surprising the combatants as they executed plans to muster and field armies. Power brokers in Europe anticipated that the war on the continent, following the declaration of war by Germany on France, would be both swift and of a decisively short duration.

European armies in 1914 were cast in the shadows of their 1870s forerunners, featuring colorful, ceremonial mounted cavalry units, horse-drawn artillery, wagon-borne supply trains, and rank-and-file foot soldiers with bayoneted muskets. There was absolutely no notion that a new era of spectacular weapons of carnage would emerge during the Great War on which they embarked. No one envisioned the level of violence, death, and destruction of the first global war. And the new, strange-looking "flying machines" had all but been ignored prior to 1914.[1]

For the most part, Americans were oblivious to the unrest in Europe, with the slight exception of the European immigrants who flooded America in the late 1800s. A prime motivation was to avoid being drafted to fight "other people's" wars, as had been the case across the continent for centuries. Post–Civil War immigrants to America concentrated along the Texas coast and in the state's central and Hill Country regions, exhibiting no desire to be involved in other people's wars (which no doubt is why they were determined to settle new lands, raise families, and farm . . . in far-off Texas)![2] Like them, the majority of Texans wanted no part of the European War.

While the casual reader picked up periodic news reports, the rank-and-file citizenry paid little or no attention to the ebb and flow of everyday European affairs. Some three dozen central Texas newspapers were printed in German and Czech and kept alive the language of the motherland in articles on local events, weather, social gatherings, and farming. Other than routine correspondence and occasional visits from relatives from the old country, these immigrants quickly adapted to Texas and were little concerned with past agitations. Instead, they focused on the news of political change across America with the recent election of a Princeton University professor, Woodrow Wilson, as president, and his not-so-veiled plans to usher in a new brand of progressivism to rein in what he considered corporate overreach and greed, both at home and abroad. How this affected the common person on the street had yet to be articulated.[3]

Wilson's campaign and planning for the presidency offered scarcely any attention or debate about European external relations or international policy changes. On election day in November 1912, the only newspaper coverage on international affairs was a shallow discussion of US dominance over, and regulation of, the Panama Canal, scheduled to open in 1914. The British, long both a commercial and naval sea power, did not want the United States to have the final say over operations and the fees charged for trans-isthmian transit. In addition, there was a secondary and vague discussion of the status of the Monroe Doctrine and the opposition to British colonialism in the Americas and the nation's intention going forward in the Western Hemisphere—a topic about which, after a careful review of the newspapers of era, I surmise most Americans had no knowledge (or cared to have any knowledge).

Wilson entered the White House with a biased, preconceived notion that industry was corrupt and heavy-handed in spreading American products, services, and influence worldwide. As a result, he objected to the actively promoted policies of his predecessor, William H. Taft, whose approach was dubbed "Dollar Diplomacy." Undoubtedly, Taft and others running the American enterprise advocated an aggressive US global business strategy that they felt benefitted the nation, and they gave the full support of the American government to the notion that "the flag" followed global trade initiatives and opened new doors to expanded foreign markets. On the competitive, global scale, this was not a new concept. The vast British Empire and, to a lesser degree, Germany and France, followed the same model to extend their national and commercial interests.[4]

Little did Wilson and his advisors realize that the very global infighting and commercial competition Europe waged on the high seas and its possessions offshore were part and parcel of the underlying tension and duplicity that enflamed the path into world war. Wilson's politically motivated appointment of serial presidential candidate William Jennings Bryan as secretary of state placed a nice, jovial man with absolutely no diplomatic or commercial experience into the job—a man who, at best, did not know the difference between central Kansas and central Europe. The entire Wilson agenda was based on a presidency occupied with a bold and insular domestic program of reform.[5]

As Wilson launched his domestic agenda, two international events abruptly upended the president's naive vision and approach to world affairs. Within days of moving into the White House, he was disarmed with a vastly out-of-control and bloody revolution in Mexico after insurgent Gen. Victoriano Huerta overthrew the government of President Francisco Madero. Wilson felt it was America's moral obligation not to recognize what was deemed a violent transfer of state power and thus began a two-year vendetta to oust Huerta. The Mexican Revolution had a tremendous impact on millions of dollars of business, banking, and industrial investments in Mexico, as well as adding grave concern for the safety of Americans working and traveling there. The Texas-Mexican border was a flashpoint of confrontations between rebel factions and Huerta's federalist troops. Hundreds of noncombatant citizens from both countries were caught in the crossfire, which on more than one occasion precipitated an armed invasion by the United States. An incident with the US Navy at Tampico, Mexico, on the Gulf of Mexico, provided the spark for the eventual American landing of troops at Vera Cruz in late April 1914. The action induced a number of Texans, including Texas Aggies, to join the Houston Light Guard, an irregular element of the state-sponsored National Guard that was deployed to the southern border under orders of Texas Governor O. B. Colquitt. All efforts toward a diplomatic and nonviolent settlement of American meddling in Mexican affairs had thus failed.[6]

Wilson's personal distrust of revolutionary leader Huerta clouded his ability to resolve the dynamics of the revolution. Violence increased in Mexico, resulting in the deaths of scores of American citizens (as well as foreign nationals) along the US-Mexico border. For nearly a decade, federalists and rebels moved along and across the border, smuggling arms and supplies, recruiting fighters, staging invasions, and discouraging cross-border trade in goods and services. Some two dozen Texas A&M cadets and alumni were called to active duty in the Texas National Guard for deployment on the Mexican border. One was future air service pioneer Herbert Molly Mason, a 1915 Texas A&M graduate who enlisted in the army as a sergeant and was assigned to the border. Even the dispatching of Gen. John J. Pershing into northern Mexico in a relentlessly dusty pursuit of rebel leader Pancho Villa yielded little success. Seeking to avoid a full-scale war between the United States and Mexico, the Wilson War Department gradually reduced the administration's level of interference with Mexico following the eruption of war in Europe. Thus, the second international crisis confronting the Wilson administration was the nation's role and involvement in the catastrophic disintegration of the nations of Europe into a deadly war.[7]

The Dogs of War

As undercurrents of the war in Europe rumbled on in 1913–1914, in what Winston Churchill (citing Shakespeare's *Julius Caesar*) called the "Dogs of

War," the Germans, French, and English increased their covert operations and overt actions south of the US border, meddling in Mexico and Latin America on the eve of the war. Their actions were veiled posturing to gain a strategic advantage in the event of an extended war in Europe and the possibility of US involvement. European nations interested in the Mexican Revolution had four primary strategic objectives, which appear from the records of the period to far exceed the projections that politicians and planners in Washington contemplated: (a) to protect foreign, private investment interests in Mexico; (b) to secure access to critical strategic petroleum supplies from Mexican oil fields; (c) to disrupt US intentions to expand into Central and South America, most notably to control the Panama Canal; and (d) to tie down the US military in the Mexican Revolution to keep US forces out of Europe. In other words, various European espionage agents manipulated Mexico in an effort to deter US intervention in the war in Europe.[8]

The show of force that the US Army was ordered to provide on the southern border in 1913 was a response to the call by governors of the border states of Texas, New Mexico, and Arizona to enforce law and order and add federal troops to protect citizens on the US side of the border. Small detachments of regular US Army troops and some support artillery were rushed to garrisons in the Texas border towns of Brownsville, Laredo,

Figure 2. Landings by Curtiss Jenny biplanes were on the main drill field across from the Academic Building. Due to the small space, many planes crashed into buildings. There were no known written reports or significant injuries. Courtesy of Cushing Memorial Library & Archives, Texas A&M University.

and El Paso. In response to the growing tensions on the border, the US Army hastily formed a provisional air unit, the 1st Aero Squadron, within the Signal Corps, stationed at Texas City, Texas, on March 5, 1913. This deployed aviation unit failed to be effective, however, due to poor equipment, inadequate training, frequent accidents, and inexperienced leadership. Interestingly, the first extensive aerial operations (bombing, close air support, and "scouting" [observation]), were conducted not by the US Army but by mercenary pilots flying for the rebel factions commanded by Pancho Villa against Mexican Federalist troops at the battle of Torreon.[9]

US Army commanders in south Texas were ordered not to shoot "unless fired upon." In Washington, the White House and State Department were to have final say on any action in Mexico or response along the border. While the United States had a diplomatic agreement with the British to investigate and represent them concerning any incident regarding their citizens, the Germans and French had no such understanding. Meanwhile, the Germans—well in advance of the famed Zimmermann diplomatic cable pledging aid to Mexico in the event of war against the United States—continued to provide arms, tactical training, financing, and military "advisors" to the Huerta government up until his fall from the presidency in July 1914.[10]

German military advisors and agents, whose role was more as spy than advisor, remained in place and very active in both the United States and Mexico to see if they could help foment a second revolution by supporting a new effort by the deposed Huerta to re-enter Mexico. German agents financed and planned Huerta's return to the Mexican border while US counterintelligence agents shadowed his every move. The old general was detained under house arrest in El Paso by US Marshals and no counter-revolution occurred, but German agents remained very active on the border for the next decade. The buildup of US Army troops, a mix of regular army and national guard units, continued on the south Texas border and grew to more than 100,000, the largest concentration of combatants since the Civil War. One additional show of force by the Americans was the dispatch of aeroplanes from the Army Signal Corps, which predated the formal organization of the Army Air Corps.[11]

Following the initial aeroplane demonstration by Wilbur Wright at Fort Myers in northern Virginia, the first use of US Army Signal Corps aeroplanes in an operational assignment was the dispatch of a 39-foot wingspan Wright Scout to Kelly Field in San Antonio in late 1909 for testing in the region's "large open space and favorable climatic conditions." The air service operation (still a subunit of the US Army Signal Corps) involved the deployment of aeroplane parts in crates by horse and wagons for assembly at Fort McIntosh, in Laredo, on the Rio Grande. They arrived in early March 1911, and, once the planes were assembled, the pilots, Lts. Benjamin D. Foulois and Philip O. Parmalee, embarked on a 106-mile-reconnaissance flight up the Rio Grande toward Eagle Pass. The sight of these low-flying planes would have created quite a stir. After a brief rest, the two pilots flew back toward Laredo but had to crash-land in the Rio Grande after engine trouble and an encounter with a flock of ducks in flight—the first military water crash and recovery. These first aeroplanes, built by the Wright brothers, had flexible wings. In addition to dodging ducks, the pilot could move his torso to reshape, or "warp," the wings using an elaborate system of wires (predating the use of ailerons), which caused the aircraft to turn. The crash-landing into the river had little impact on Foulois's military career. By 1917, he was promoted to the rank of brigadier general and appointed chief of the Army Air Service in France. The planes he and Parmalee wrecked were recovered, packed into wagons in Laredo, and returned to San Antonio. Later in the revolution, there were reports of private contractors flying in Mexico, as well as Air Service reconnaissance flights during the 1916–1917 Pershing campaign. The Wright aircraft would have made a tremendous impression wherever it traveled.[12]

Wings Over Aggieland

In early December 1911, less than eight years after the Wright Brothers made their historic 1903 flights at Kitty Hawk, North Carolina, a fragile, single-stroke engine "Wright Flyer" piloted by Lt. Robert G. Fowler circled the Texas A&M campus and landed on Kyle Field, coming to a full stop precisely on the gridiron 50-yard line. While Texas newspapers had reported on manned balloon flights and other aviation advances since the mid-1890s, this stunt amazed those in attendance and to this day ranks among the most historic flights and landings in the state of Texas. Its historical significance was vividly captured by Texas A&M archivist David Chapman '67 in the monograph *Wings Over Aggieland* (1994):[13]

> At 1:37 on the afternoon of December 1, 1911, the aviation age, with all its dreams, hopes and promises for the future, sputtered onto Kyle Field

Figure 3. The first airplane landing in College Station was on Kyle Field on December 1, 1911, and created a great deal of excitement for aviation among the Aggie cadets. Pilot Robert Fowler guided his Wright Flyer to a full stop on the 50-yard line. Courtesy of Cushing Memorial Library & Archives, Texas A&M University.

at the Agricultural and Mechanical College of Texas. The event was of such importance that citizens ceased their daily activities all along the flight path to gaze skyward hoping to catch a glimpse of the little biplane making its way through the valley of the Brazos River to the campus at A&M. Reports of Fowler's fragile little craft were dispatched quickly along the route. In Bryan, the telegraph operator received word that Fowler had left Hearne at 12:45 following the railroad tracks, and would land at the College to refuel. The news spread like wildfire throughout the town. All business and social activity came to a halt as people poured into the streets to see a craft that they had only read about in newspapers. At 1:15 p.m. a small white speck became visible in the clear, bright, blue winter sky. As the craft flew closer, the crowd could see the spinning propeller and hear the far-off popping of the little engine.

At 1:20, Fowler's machine was clearly visible to the eager throng of students and faculty members gathered to watch the arrival of the first aircraft ever on campus. Over the campus, Fowler slowly circled Kyle Field and the aircraft "alighted gracefully as a bird." More than 400 students rushed toward the little aircraft to stare in amazement and disbelief. Some hesitantly touched the craft as if to prove it was real and not fantasy. Lt. Fowler, trained by Orville and Wilber Wright, had lunch with the cadets, refueled the aircraft, and took off at 3 p.m. "into the cerulean blue."

In the short span of a few hours, the College had seen the "birdman" and begun a love affair with aviation that would marry the school's strong technical background to the mysteries of flight.

The allure of aviation predated the Kyle Field landing and continued long after. As early as April 1911, the committee coordinating the spring banquet of the Ross Volunteers cadet organization assembled and suspended a fragile facsimile of the Wright Flyer from the ceiling of the old Mess Hall. The bi-plane, "with propellers going," was filled with red and blue balloons as the centerpiece of the annual dance. Following the grand march and procession of cadets and guests, the "airship made a descent" to drop the balloons! But what proved the greatest thrill involved the vivid display by aviation pioneers of the day. The editors of the 1913 Texas A&M yearbook, the *Longhorn*, also noted their fascination with flight, airbrushing an aeroplane above the main flagpole in a photograph over the heart of campus.[14]

Excitement over flight continued to build, although most Texans had never seen an aeroplane. Visiting "barnstormers"—some dubbed the "world's greatest birdmen" by the *Bryan Daily Eagle*—performed aerial stunts for enthusiastic College Station and Bryan crowds at Dellwood Amusement Park and Race Track along the interurban trolley line that connected the college with Bryan, passing what later became Cavitt Street

Figure 4. This picture from the 1913 *Longhorn* yearbook is an early example of "photo-shopping" an image with the addition of French Bleriot Monoplane designed by Louis Bleriot over the center of campus. 1913 *Longhorn* yearbook, courtesy of Cushing Memorial Library & Archives, Texas A&M University.

Figure 5. Many Texas A&M cadets received their first introduction to flight in Dell-wood Park two miles north of the campus. Pictured in 1915 is the French Bleriot monoplane of stunt pilot Harold Kantner. Courtesy of Cushing Memorial Library & Archives, Texas A&M University.

two miles north of the college. Cadets were able to get close to both the airplanes and the pilots as each new visiting aerial troupe pushed the en-velope to fly higher and faster. These "speed demons" of the air, among them Harold Kantner, as Chapman noted, looked to impress onlookers as well as to chase speed records that reached 105 miles per hour by 1914, thanks to a 70-horsepower Gnome engine, considered enormous at the time. These prewar private aviators in America, using French-designed aircraft, were significantly ahead of the fledging US Air Service. Thus, this early era of flight, driven by speed and altitude, emboldened an entire generation of future aviators. Much like many of the early dreamers of flight, it is very possible, but not confirmed, that a number of the young cadets in the large crowd around the Wright Flyer on Kyle Field that cool December afternoon were inspired by the winged landing to become some of Texas A&M's first aviators in World War I.[15]

And so, a new chapter in American military history was about to un-fold—yet not, at first, with aviation. As historian Samuel Hynes noted, "in the summer of 1914 there wasn't yet an air war to go to."[16]

Early Texas Aggie Volunteers

Shortly after the opening salvos of the 1914 "guns of August" that pro-pelled Europe into war, and despite the fact that there was a vocal antiwar opinion across America against any sort of involvement, eager volunteers from the United States booked ocean transit to England and France to enlist in the military. Dozens of Texas Aggies were no exception. Even today, it is difficult to comprehend the magnitude of carnage and destruction they witnessed. The Great War was more than half over when the American army officially arrived in mid-1917. During the first 36 months of the war, over 5 million had been killed in the bloody stalemate on the Western Front—an astonishing 5,000 deaths per day. It is difficult to document the exact number of early enlistees, but records are becoming more available that chronicle a clearer picture of early American activity prior to the official US entry in the war after the declaration on April 6, 1917.[17]

The first pre-1917 arrivals of volunteer Americans in Europe joined the British and French armies. Some enlisted as ambulance drivers, doctors, or foot-soldiers, and many of the most eager and adventurous were dispatched to the French Foreign Legion. There was little fanfare, and the process to join was very easy. The Texas A&M *Alumni Directory* expressed concern about the accuracy of its information regarding former students serving in the foreign armies, noting that a number are "somewhere in France." Those who did indicate their early service included Dr. John Ashton '06, a veterinarian with the First Veterinary Hospital in the British Expeditionary Force, who in later years penned a famous Aggie Muster poem, and Dr. Bertus Clyde Ball '13, who served as a surgeon in the French army. Lt. Nat S. Perrine '17, who enlisted and fought with the Fourth French Army, received the Croix de Guerre for gallantry in action. Upon completion of his tour in the French army, Perrine was commissioned in the US Army, rising to the rank of general in World War II, one of six general officers from the Texas A&M Class of '17.[18]

One of the most remarkable early Aggies to join the fighting on the Verdun line was a young civil engineering graduate from Houston, Georges P. F. Jouine '07. Working on a levy construction project on the Mississippi River when the war broke out in France, he paid his way to Paris, enlisted in the army, and soon received a battlefield promotion as an officer. The short war promised by the recruiters was not to be, however, and Jouine served 34 months on the front lines. Wounded six times, he was known to have been one of the earliest pioneers of an early, revolutionary new war machine: the tank. As a tank commander in early 1916, he developed and tested tactical maneuvers and mobility strategies that in future wars would make this weapon even more deadly. In all, he received over a dozen decorations from three nations and is the most decorated Texas A&M former student of WWI. After the war, Jouine returned to Houston and the engineering profession as the president of the Gladys City Oil Company and honorary consul for France in Texas. In 1958, in recognition of Jouine's many achievements, the Corps of Cadets named the annual award for the most outstanding scholastic cadet unit the "Jouine Award."[19]

One of the earliest Air Service pioneers and among the first Texas A&M aviators was Lt. Douglas B. Netherwood '08, who transferred from the Coastal Artillery Corps to the "aero corps" in late 1913. Shortly after the War Department purchased an airplane, a Wright Flyer Model C, he joined the Army Aviation School and the 1st Aero Squadron at North Island, in San Diego, California, considered the army's first operational aviation unit. Netherwood arrived on the West Coast just as the army, aware of aerial advances in Europe, addressed three looming challenges: (a) no suitable planes to fly, (b) not enough pilots to fly them, and (c) an urgent need to test and improve all aspects of next-generation planes for the Aviation [Air] Service of the Signal Corps of the US Army. Civilian observers and the press were aware of these challenges and noted the pilot shortage and inferior aircraft as astonishing news given the advances in aviation as the air war unfolded over Europe. The *Aerial Age Weekly* noted the obvious aviation technology lag in America, stating that to train a "first-class operator [pilot] takes something like six months." Time was not on the side of the early efforts to develop a US Army Air Service.[20]

Lt. Netherwood, a mechanical engineering major, was among the first in military aviation to test aircraft and conduct "experimental trials" to improve the range, speed, and operational capabilities of the planes the Air Service had on hand, as well as to evaluate new models as quickly as possible for service. Working with civilian flight instructor Francis A. Wildman, Netherwood was placed in charge of the chase cars that followed the airborne "machines" under evaluation to "take notes." Their first duty assignment, apparently not affected by the meager aviation service budget at the time, was to choose suitable autos for the "chase." After "a strenuous comparative test of nearly all the American [automobile] makers" that offered cars able to travel long distances under harsh conditions, he purchased two 1913 Hupmobile Roadsters. For the next few months, Netherwood and Wildman criss-crossed southern California, logging their data on flight tests in late 1915. Netherwood then was assigned to the signal corps aviation element in the Philippines, and even after the crash of the only available plane into Manila Bay, he remained there until transferred to Love Field in Dallas to oversee aviation logistics services. Evaluation and the assessment of new aircraft and support systems also was carried out at Aberdeen Proving Grounds in Washington, staffed by over a dozen A&M former students from 1917 to 1919. These test flights helped usher in tremendous changes in American aviation design, endurance, and functional capabilities. Change and innovation driven by real-time needs would come at a rapid pace. In the course of the First World War, as aviation historian Eric Lawson noted, airspeeds doubled, maximum altitudes and climb rates tripled, typical engine power increased fivefold, machine gunfire rates went up by 10 times, and bomb loads increased a hundred-fold.[21]

Texas Aggies were part of what started as an informal call to arms that helped spread the growing craze for aviation nationwide. Organized groups of students and alumni at nonmilitary universities privately began to sponsor such groups as the Harvard Flying Corps in Boston; the Curtiss Flying School in Buffalo, New York; the First Yale Unit [and Aero Club] in New Haven; and the Princeton Aero Club in New Jersey, touted as the "Aviation Corps of Princeton University." The allure of flying quickly enthralled members of these volunteer organizations. One of the earliest aviation spectacles of the prewar era was performed prior to the Princeton-Yale football game on November 18, 1916: the first pregame "fly-over," unofficially dubbed "The Football Special." The flight was composed of a fleet of twelve slow-moving aeroplanes. Led by Capt. Reynal C. Bolling, the Mineola, New York, unit of the National Guard, according to *The New York Times*, dazzled the crowd, as the pilots "dipped, spiraled, and looped-the-loop, and each daring manoeuvre [sic] brought the crowd to their feet and evoked prolonged cheers." Widely publicized, this event was not without one lost plane, one falling out with engine trouble, and one crash-landing on the outskirts of Princeton. These eager young members of the aero clubs would be among the first aviators to fly in combat in France.[22]

Rough Tough! Real Stuff!

In the spring of 1917, following the declaration of war, A&M administrators urged cadets to remain enrolled and await notification of their military status. As debate on the possibility of American involvement in the war grew, it became clear to many that they soon would be called to active duty. All the regular army officers assigned to military training on campus had been recalled to active military units, including cadet commandant Col. C. H. Muller and his assistant, Lt. W. H. Morris. A&M College President William Bizzell offered all the available campus facilities to the US War Department for training and housing recruits, noting with pride that, "after forty years the military instruction at the A&M College has received ample vindication and [is] justified by those who succeeded in including military science as a required subject in the land-grant college." Furthermore, in advance of the declaration of war, Bizzell moved quickly to urge (and there is indication that he did so with the tacit endorsement of US Army officials) increased funding from the Texas legislature in order to be prepared in the event of a rapid troop mobilization, noting, "The crisis in international affairs will compel the college to expand facilities in these serious times." The college soon received additional funding for training facilities and barracks.[23]

Spirts were high on the A&M campus as first-season football coach Dana X. Bible finished the greatest single season in the college's sports history, compiling an undefeated record of eight wins and no losses, with the team scoring 270 points while holding every opponent scoreless. In spite of the war planning, the Corps of Cadets continued its "Corps trips" for football games at Baylor University in Waco and Rice Institute in Houston, each of which included a grand parade through the city. Little did the Aggie players and coach realize that they would soon be in uniform for duty "over there." In Texas, as well as across the country, the full impact of the burgeoning war in Europe had not yet been realized or appreciated, nor was its ultimate toll on American involvement anticipated. The first detachment of US Army troops of the American Expeditionary Force (AEF) arrived in France on June 26, 1917. By Christmas 1917, most of the A&M cadet members of the championship football and basketball teams, along with Coach Bible, were either training to go to France or were already on duty there.[24]

In terms of America's preparation for war, the country was at the lowest state of readiness in its history. The hundreds of cadets trained at the A&M College prior to the war were relegated to periodic activity with volunteer militia groups organized across the state that were little more than ceremonial honor guard units. The professional US Army officer corps had been reduced to the minimum needed, the pay was poor, promotion in rank was slow, and there were no retirement programs. The brief Spanish-American War was fought hastily and primarily with volunteer-militia units that the army quickly deactivated as soon as Teddy Roosevelt's "splendid little war" was over. Of the nearly 100 Texas Aggies who served briefly in Cuba and the Philippines from 1898 to 1901, only about a dozen army officers trained and commissioned at Texas A&M remained on active duty after 1900.

Limited US-Mexican border duty by the US Army and Texas militia followed after the beginning of the 1910 revolution. The Pershing Punitive Expedition into Mexico in 1916 stretched the army's resources to the point of collapse. And except for some Air Service reconnaissance flight operations flying Curtiss JN-3s (known as Jennies) in support of Pershing's chase after Pancho Villa, the army had no formal air operations. The aviation section had been attached to the Army Signal Corps—thus receiving no funding or recognition. Aviation had a very limited impact on army warfare doctrine before the United States entered WWI and was downplayed by the army as little more than a support role for "observation" or reconnaissance, couriers, and airborne charged with spotting the direction of artillery fire units.[25]

Figure 6. James Knox Walker in his plane during World War I. Courtesy of Walker family.

Most of the early Texas A&M aviators began their careers on the ground. Lt. John W. "Billie" Butts '10 had transferred from the cavalry to the air service and earned his wings at San Diego in January 1916, then flew missions in Mexico with the ill-equipped First Aero Squadron at Columbus, New Mexico. And following graduation in the A&M Class of '15, Herbert M. Mason joined the army as a sergeant in the Pershing Expedition and future aviator. On the eve of the US declaration of war in early April 1917, the Army Air Section nationwide consisted of 65 officers (many not certified to fly), some 1,000 support personnel, and about a dozen Martin Model TT training planes (maximum speed 96 miles per hour), of which the Army Inspector General noted, "none are considered fit for service in battle."[26]

The first Texas Aggie aviator in the Great War was Sergeant Herbert Mason '15, who traded his dusty experiences in the cavalry to volunteer with the first 50 cadets to go overseas in late 1916 to learn to fly with the British Royal Air Corps. Upon completion of pilot training on the ARVO 504 (and numerous early models), earning his wings and being commissioned as a lieutenant, he remained in the Royal Air Force (RAF) assigned to the British 1st "Defense of London" Squadron. The RAF mission was primarily an effort to interdict German attacks on British urban areas and English Channel shipping. Additionally, he was among the first Americans to fly support flights in the single-engine Nieuport 27, followed by night bombing missions in the Handley-Page bombers of the Northern Bombing Group over Germany. Mason would fly missions the entire war and after Armistice became part of the organization of the 111th Observation Squadron of the 36th Air Force.[27]

The American declaration of war in April 1917 was but a formality as the United States had broken off all diplomatic relations with Germany in February 1917 following the renewal of an unrestricted Atlantic submarine campaign that began to sink unarmed American and allied merchants. These German U-boat attacks tipped the scales on drawing America into the war. Having won reelection with the slogan that he would "keep America out of the European war," Wilson soon faced the need to mobilize and train an extensive armed forces to soon fight "over there." In May 1917, President Wilson selected Maj. Gen. John J. Pershing to command the first AEF. Interestingly, having led the Mexican Punitive Expedition, a generally frustrating cat-and-mouse game in the dust, sand, and heat of northern Mexico, the new general expressed reservations from his head-quarters at Fort Sam Houston a few days after his appointment, noting, "it will be necessary to train the [troops] in the 'new-fangled' method of trench warfare." The intuition of the general, who had never seen the maze of trenches on the Western Front, would soon be verified.[28]

General Pershing's command experience with around 20,000 horse-mounted troops on the Mexican border provided little precedent for the size and complexity of the armies that would become the AEF and ultimately comprise nearly one-third of all Allied troops on the Western Front. Two months after the declaration of war, American citizens began registering for the draft, and by September 1918, more than 24 million men—nearly half of all male Americans of draft age—had signed up. Ultimately, some 4.1 million men and women were inducted into service, of which 20 percent were foreign-born immigrants.[29]

Correspondingly, the quiet, rural A&M College of Texas campus was about to undergo the greatest transformation in its brief history. The four decades of solid-grounded military training by the Corps of Cadets since 1876 was an integral part of cadet life and academics and was largely re-sponsible for the college's public image. While cadets at A&M received training in the basics of military tactics, leadership, marksmanship, and protocol, few former students, until WWI, had served on active duty. This preparation was soon to justify the letter and spirit of the federal Morrill Act of 1862 that laid the foundation for a tradition of "citizen soldiers" to answer the nation's call to arms.[30]

> You've no idea how beautiful the earth is from a mile's height in the air. Roads look like little white scars, trees look like little green bumps, fields like beautiful little pin-cushions, buildings like orderly little blocks that you build toy-houses with, the water like flashing sap-phires, and the fine cool air—just as fresh as that in the mountains.
> —Lt. Hal Irby Greer 'x95

2

CALL TO ARMS

The declaration of war caused us to realize that we were going to be compelled to modify our plans. The military training that our student has received made them very important factors in the war plans and as a result practically every member of the senior class [of '17] had left the college in order to accept service in the war.

—Nester M. McGinnis '08
A&M College Alumni Secretary: May 1917

But there is one element in relation to the flying machine that we are not producing . . . and that is the men. We can produce machines, but not the aviators. That takes time. Where will we get the men, and where are we to train them?

—Alexander Graham Bell, April 1916

Mobilization on the home front in the face of concerned public opposition to any involvement in the European war was a major challenge to the Wilson Administration. German threats on the high seas in the North Atlantic (as well as unreported, covert German espionage activity in Mexico geared to disrupt operations in the United States) would soften the mobilization and transition to rearming. The president was not completely without focus on some degree of planning and preparation, signing the landmark National Defense Act of June 3, 1916, which expanded both the army and navy—and, more importantly, created the Reserve Officer Training Program [or Corps], or ROTC. One key purpose of this action was to increase the size of the army by authorizing an increase in the number of commissioned officers from 5,029 to 11,327. The new officer training and commissioning program was fully embraced by Texas A&M and complemented the institution's historical military orientation. While few officers were commissioned under the new ROTC programs during World War I, due to the lateness of its implementation prior to the armistice, the college would emerge from the war with an enhanced focus on professional military education, which continues to this day and a hallmark of which is the annual campus commissioning ceremonies of hundreds of citizen-soldiers in all branches of the armed forces.[1]

In the decade prior to the war, the A&M College campus gradually addressed growth and enhancement of programs in line with its mandate to train students in engineering and agricultural disciplines. Following

Figure 7. Prewar picture of the Texas A&M campus taken in 1916 from atop the water tank. (1) Main Building, (2) Electrical Engineering, (3) Goodwin Hall, (4) Old Assembly Hall, (5) YMCA, (6) Foster Hall, (7) Dormitory, (8) Ross Hall, (9) Dormitory, (10) Machine Shop, (11) drill field and future runway for airplanes, (12) athletic field, (13) gymnasium, (14) Austin Hall, (15) pointing to railroad station, and (16) Military Walk. Author's collection.

the death of Gen. Lawrence Sullivan Ross in early 1898, the college would have three presidents prior to the appointment of David F. Houston, former dean of faculty at the University of Texas, in April 1902. Houston was very effective in enhancing the curriculum, attracting new faculty, and lobbying the legislature in Austin to expand campus facilities to allow for growth. He raised the college entrance age from 15 to 16 and expanded entry exam procedures. His efforts reached fruition after his departure to become president of the University of Texas in September 1905, with the addition of two new dorms, Goodwin and Milner Halls, to ease overcrowding by moving cadets out of temporary tents into improved quarters. He also oversaw the erection of the Civil Engineering Building and the construction of the Agricultural Experiment Station Building, which served as the headquarters for the dispersal of research enhancements, production improvements, and extension programs to assist scores of farmers and ranchers statewide.[2]

In August 1908, Robert T. Milner began what would turn out to be six years as A&M's president. In addition to the formal establishment of the Schools of Agriculture and Engineering, he presided over the construction of the two largest projects and facilities since the founding of the college in 1876: the Academic Building (1914, $225,000) to replace Old Main, which was destroyed by fire in May 1912, and Sbisa Mess Hall (1915, $205,000) to replace the old Mess Hall, also destroyed by fire, on November 11, 1911 The continued growth of the Corps of Cadets was addressed with the addition of Leggett and Mitchell Halls. From 1910 until America's entry in the war in 1917, student enrollment at Texas A&M averaged over 1,000 cadets each academic year. Milner's departure in late 1913 opened the way for William B. Bizzell to become president. The ROTC (supplanted by the Student Army Training Corps [SATC] was open to all men over 18. The college's military orientation, a mandate of the Morrill Land-Grant Act under which it was founded just after the Civil War, would prove a critical component on the eve of America's entry into war. As noted by Henry Dethloff, "Texas A&M fully embraced the military training programs which so thoroughly complemented the institution's historic military orientation . . . the mark of the military now became an indelible part of Texas A&M tradition."[3]

By the November 1918 armistice, more than 190,000 Texans, including more than 2,300 Texas Aggies, served in the armed services. Those in uniform were supported on the home front by contributions from thousands of Texans from all sectors of the state's economy. In addition to food production, Texas provided cotton that was the source of over 400 miles (some 800 million yards) of khaki fabric. War production included extensive oil and gas products, arms and munitions manufacturing, and trainloads of east Texas lumber. Texans also responded by organizing a vast network of localized Red Cross, YMCA, and Salvation Army services and activities. In response to the call from Washington to support the war efforts, Texas (the fifth largest state in terms of population) was a leader in War Bond drives to assist the government in funding the expanding war. The state was predominately rural. Its four largest cities, each over 100,000 in population, were San Antonio, Dallas, Houston, and Fort Worth. The population of Austin ranked tenth among Texas cities, with 33,000 citizens. The extensive Texas contribution to the Allied victory is noted by military historian Robert Wooster: "The mobilization of the mind and spirit of Texas during the First World War kindled the growth of patriotism and Americanism," bringing Texans—who primarily viewed themselves as "Southerners'"into the mainstream of the nation's life.[4]

The Big Oak Tree

World War I was to be a major watershed in the history of Texas A&M. The number of changes and enhancements to campus facilities, as well as the growth in scope and quality of educational programs and research, can be dated from this period. In this regard, President Bizzell, who assumed the presidency on September 19, 1914, would prove to be an active visionary and energetic leader. Upon entering the presidency, he had the support of the board of directors and the Texas legislature to make improvements and additions to the facilities on campus. The YMCA building was completed in early 1915 and the Animal Judging Pavilion in late 1916. In 1917, after years of planning, Guion Hall, with seating for 2,500, was built for assemblies and graduation; headquarters for the Engineering Experiment Station and a four-story veterinary medicine building, later named Francis Hall, added to the changing campus skyline. A new dormitory, as well as a new power generation facility and telephone connections to support campus growth, were begun on the eve of the war.[5]

Once the number of Atlantic U-boat sinkings increased and the top-secret Zimmermann Telegram (on Germany's efforts to use Mexico as a base of operations against America) became public, there was little doubt that America would soon engage in the war "over there." On March 23, 1917, in advance of the formal declaration of war, Bizzell and the board of directors offered the entire A&M campus facilities and staff to assist with federal wartime training needs, making it the first institution in the nation to step forward.

Texas A&M College Board Resolution

Whereas, the President and the Congress of the United States are confronted with a serious international crisis that may at any time result in a declaration of war; and

Whereas, the Agricultural and Mechanical College of Texas is a land-grant institution established by an act of Congress in 1862 presumably for the purpose of preparing men for military service and technical pursuits: and

Whereas, the conditions of modern warfare demand technical trained men for military service, therefore, be it:

> Resolved, that we, the Faculty of the Agricultural and Mechanical College of Texas, earnestly request the immediate approval of the Board of Directors, sanctioned if necessary by the Legislature of Texas, for the rendering to the Federal government of all research and instructional facilities of this College, the same to be subject to the direction of the Secretaries of War and Navy, and that we hereby, individually and collectively, pledge our support to the international policies of the Federal government and earnestly request the Governor and Legislature of this State to assume undiminished the continuance of appropriations during the continuance of such Federal use irrespective of the suspension of the instructional functions of any or all of the College departments. We urge the favorable consideration of this resolution by the Board of Directors of the College and if necessary by the legislature also.

Minutes of the Texas A&M College Board of Directors, March 23, 1917, III, pp. 212–213

Bizzell, who had no military experience, nevertheless had a solid grasp of the urgency of the situation. He constantly reminded the cadets, faculty, and public that, in this war effort, everyone—students, faculty, farmers, engineers, priests, and ministers—was a soldier.[6] Quite possibly, Bizzell was influenced by the venerable Dean Edwin J. Kyle '99, who questioned the general lack of national preparedness and the need (and obligation) for the A&M College to be an example of patriotism and dedicated service. From April 1917 to early 1919, the A&M campus was on a "war footing," fully mobilized to expand facilities and house trainees to plan, prepare, and train for the war. Bizzell, with extreme pride, informed all that the selection of A&M, after extensive meetings and accolades in Washington, DC, was with just cause, stating that "The unusual proficiency of the Agricultural and Mechanical College men immediately attracted the favorable attention of the officers of the Army and won them the confidence and esteem of the highest military experts in our country."[7]

The impact on the Corps of Cadets was immediate and long-lasting. Prior to the formal declaration of war, cadets had been urged to remain in their classes. This abruptly changed with Wilson's declaration of war. The majority of the A&M cadet Class of 1917 were excused from their final academic classes by early May and ordered by the US Army to Camp Funston, Leon Spring, Texas, for the first officer training course under the command of Col. William Scott, the former A&M commandant of cadets in the late 1880s. As the remaining members of the junior class of '18 began to volunteer to enlist directly into the armed forces, Bizzell received special permission from the War Department to allow qualified cadets to join the officer candidate group at Leon Springs. Within weeks, more than 100 buildings were constructed at the new camp—barracks, a mess hall, training and administrative centers, a hospital, and an assembly hall—to accommodate some 1,500 officer candidates.[8]

With the exodus of A&M cadets into officer training and enlistments, the traditional routine of the campus was abruptly transformed with the implementation of on-campus War Department training programs. One challenge facing Bizzell was adequate campus staffing. Over two dozen faculty and staff resigned their positions to volunteer for active duty. Thus, the June 1917 campus commencement ceremonies were canceled and moved by Bizzell and the A&M board of directors to "under a big oak tree" at Leon Springs, where diplomas were awarded to 73 of the 136 cadets in the Class of '17, irrespective of their inability to fully complete all end-of-semester course work due to the call to active duty. President Bizzell proudly noted, "I could not find it in my heart to let these boys receive their degrees without some semblance of commencement exercises. When we saw that we could not have our boys with us in June we decided to bring commencement to them at the camp." These former cadets, and hundreds to follow from the A&M College, contributed to every Army branch of the military establishment, including the infantry, field artillery, aviation service, cavalry, and signal corps as well as the US Navy, Marines, and Coast Guard. One noticeable mark of change occurred in September 1917, when the Corps of Cadets put away the old, traditional gray, gold-and-black trimmed uniforms worn since the college opened in 1876 and donned US-Army-issue khaki and olive drab with cavalry-style campaign hats.[9]

Mechanics for Pershing's Army

Enrollment in the A&M Corps of Cadets dropped from nearly 1,300 cadets in May 1917 to under 900 in late 1918. Many faculty resigned to accept more lucrative jobs elsewhere or to join the army. As cadets and staff departed for new assignments, President Bizzell and the A&M staff prepared for the influx of new army and navy trainees in mid-1918. The National Committee on Defense was established to craft plans and programs in conjunction with War Department representatives for the SATC. The SATC program allowed cadets enrolled in A&M who were over 18 years of age to register for the draft, immediately be inducted into the service as a "private" with base pay, and return to college classes in preparation for being sent to one of the Army Officer Training programs. If there was any doubt regarding the seriousness of the situation facing the cadets, however, College Dean Charles Puryear advised the cadets, faculty, former students, and families, in a feature article in the *Alumni Quarterly*, that cadets in the new SATC programs were "subject to call [to active duty] at any time, should the exigencies of the military situation demand it."[10]

On-campus US Army training classes were organized as detachments and identified by military service and the nature of the specialty training received. Training ranged from the basic skills of farriers—experts in horseshoeing and hoof care—to advanced aviation electronics and meteorology. Daily, groups of military inductees arrived by the Houston and Texas Central train from Houston or Dallas for intensive coursework ranging from 28 days to 24 weeks. Housed in hastily built barracks, renovated animal stables, and conference training rooms, civilian War Department staff, as well as active duty army and naval personnel, worked closely with A&M professor Francis C. Bolton, director of War Education. The majority of enlistees were under the command of six US Army Infantry officers and a medical officer. Instruction was developed and presented jointly by A&M staff and military personnel. The mens' only belongings were their army-issued uniforms and a duffel bag. Once the specialized training on campus was completed, the army assigned the troops to repair and logistical units or as mechanics in aviation squadrons across the nation for either immediate duty or further training prior to deployment to Europe.

By March 1918, over 3,000 American mechanics, including hundreds who were trained at the A&M College, were shipped to England to work and train with the British aviation and arms industry or directly with the Royal Air Force. Once this orientation phase was complete, airmen were assigned to an air service aero squadron and transferred to France.[11]

Figure 8. Training outside of the Animal Husbandry Pavilion included expanded traditional instruction in the farrier program, as thousands of horses were a major form of transportation throughout World War I in France. Courtesy of Cushing Memorial Library & Archives, Texas A&M University.

Table 1. Sample of World War I special training at Texas A&M, 1917–1918

Number of Trainees	Specialty
1,731	Auto mechanics and vulcanizers
1,305	Company K: Signal Corps
340	"Buzzer" practice—communication
338	Meteorological school
320	Radio electricians
100	Naval steam engine machines
86	Blacksmiths and horseshoers (*sic*)
18	Surveyors and topographical
6	General mechanics

Source: *A&M College Bulletin*, June 1, 1918, and June 1, 1919.

Some 4,000 military personnel passed through the A&M campus during the first year, creating a strain on staffing and facilities. Campus dorms, as well as available, local Bryan housing, were strained to overflowing. To address housing needs, nine two-story barrack buildings (140 × 42 feet), a canteen, and a 1,300-seat annex section added to the mess hall were constructed. Soon, 16-hour days were the norm as campus dining hall steward Bernard Sbisa worked around the clock to daily feed twice the number the mess hall ordinarily accommodated. Cadets and incoming trainees were trained and soon transferred for additional military orientation to locations all over the country and then to East Coast troop-holding "depots" for transport overseas. The first contingent of cadets under the new ROTC program attended a four-week summer camp at Fort Sheridan, Illinois. In June 1918, many cadets remained at camp to receive additional training followed by a commission in September.[12]

Academics in the traditional sense had been displaced since most civilians and soldiers "had their hearts and minds in the war." The small number of teenage freshmen and sophomores in the Corps of Cadets, dubbed the "Kiddy Korps," were left on campus to pursue academic courses until ready for duty. The traditional, dress gray cadet uniforms were retired in exchange for the olive drab (and khaki) issue of the US Army. The new army-issue uniforms were intended to facilitate rapid transition from cadet life to the army. The new army uniform was to be used on active duty and required only a change out of the cadet's rank and shoulder patch for that of the regular army assignment. Cadet life was turned upside down by the army, navy, and SATC training demands and schedule. Chapel attendance, mandatory since the college opened in the fall of 1876, was no longer compulsory. Student publications such as the *Battalion* newspaper, *Longhorn* yearbook, and *Reveille* monthly staff newsletter were briefly suspended in the fall of 1918. The exodus of cadets to military duty prior to formal graduation grew, with those who were short the requirements for official graduation receiving an "Honor War Certificate."[13]

The Pavilion

While flight training was not conducted directly at the college, planes landed daily on the main drill field in front of the YMCA building to deliver staff and equipment from Ellington Field south of Houston, Love

Figure 9. The Texas A&M campus was transformed to support the training programs of the US armed forces. Aviation training at the college was offered in the converted Animal Husbandry Pavilion, today located next to Evans Library. The facility was cleaned and converted into an aviation hanger for instruction in engine, radio, and fuselage repair. Courtesy of Cushing Memorial Library & Archives, Texas A&M University.

Field in Dallas, and Kelly Field in San Antonio. Cadets and army trainees
were host to the spectacle of biplanes landing and taxiing across campus,
past the Academic Building eastward a short distance to the repurposed
Animal Husbandry Pavilion. Agricultural engineering professor LeRoy
Rhodes, who would resign his job at A&M to join the air service, recalled
that as many as seven planes per day came and went from campus.[14]

Cadets and army personnel saw the planes up close—sometimes too
close. In what seemed to be a regular occurrence, those in daily training
witnessed a number of aviation accidents on the main campus. There was
no control tower or direct communication with in-bound pilots. Some
planes overshot the drill field and, with little braking, ended up nose-
down in the dirt. And, on a number of occasions, planes crashed into trees
and bushes on take-off. There was little or no investigation of these inci-
dents, and no known records of them exist. To the amazement of bystand-
ers, pilots generally walked or limped away from their planes with a few
cuts and occasional broken bones. The candor and fearless approach to
flying is reflected in the words of one pilot:[15]

> An airman can usually tell when a crash is inevitable, and he must make
> up his mind how he can use his undercarriage of the plane if necessary
> to best advantage, first of all to save the life of his observer and his own,
> and, if possible, to save the engine, the most valuable part of the machine.
>
> He may have to "pancake" into a patch or bush, or he may have to
> fly deliberately between two trees and strip his wings, but so long as he
> keeps his head the chances of making a successful crash are greatly in his
> favor.

Originally a holding area for livestock and a site for animal science and
veterinary classes, the large, red-brick, high-ceilinged Pavilion (which
stands today) was cleared out, the stalls removed, the floor cleaned and
packed, and an overhead hoist added to lift and move aircraft fuselages,
engines, and wings. High bay windows allowed ample light during the
daylight-to-dusk training schedule. Adjacent horse stables were converted
into mechanical shops, classrooms, and storage. The damp, winter days
of 1917–1918 and poor ventilation failed to reduce the stale-earthy, bo-
vine "smells" and provided a clear reminder to all regarding the Pavilion's
original purpose.

The training day began with formation and roll call, followed by break-
fast at Sbisa Dining Hall. Cadets and trainees ate all three meals in shifts.

Outside mealtime, the cadets and trainees ran a parallel schedule as the cadets concentrated on academic classes and the army students on their specialized, single-purpose courses. Housing remained crowded even after the addition of new barracks in the fall of 1917, yet the turnover of trainees was constant and measured in weeks once their course was completed. With limited access to automobiles, cadets and trainees traveled the four or so miles to Bryan on the narrow-gauge Interurban Trolley that ran north along Cavitt Street. The H&TC railroad added extra trains to the schedule for College Station and along its entire north-south network.[16]

Campus social activities also were greatly curtailed, often limited to intramural baseball and, in the fall 1917 and 1918, football games. While the campus was on a wartime footing beginning in April 1917, it was not until Thanksgiving and the second wave of departures (after the mass induction of the Class of '17) with the exodus of cadets, staff, and faculty to the ranks that all involved realized the massive changes coming over the college. President Bizzell constantly petitioned the War Department for additional funding for housing and expansion of the hospital and mess hall. The military mobilization priorities in Washington, DC, however, focused on support of the troops in France and England, not on the requirements and demands of the college.

As Gen. J. J. "Blackjack" Pershing awaited in France the balance of the army and navy to arrive from the States in the latter half of 1917, he had three main priorities: to staff, train, and equip the US Army, as well as establish his field command headquarters. Furthermore, efforts were ongoing by the American Expeditionary Force (AEF) to prevent the Allies (i.e., the French and British) from gaining control over its troops and commanding them piecemeal in combat, while at the same time developing the logistical support and communications needed to support the AEF in the field. These objectives required many levels of planning and coordination on a scale previously unheard of. Pershing first assigned a freshly minted major, George C. Marshall, with the task of developing and coordinating troop training. For the chief role of the critical organization of logistics and transportation, he assigned Texas Aggie Col. Edward B. Cushing '80, of Houston.

Cushing, who served as manager for the Southern Pacific Railroad for three decades, played a major role in the AEF logistics and transportation. A very successful railroad executive and businessman, and by 1915 an avid

Figure 10. Edward B. Cushing '80 (Class of 1880) was one of the first cadets at the A&M College of Texas. Prior to the war he was active in organizing the Ex-Cadets Association, forerunner of the Association of Former Students, and was a member of the A&M board of directors and a senior manager of railroad operations in Texas. Joining the army at 56 years old, he was immediately promoted to the rank of major and was in charge of all logistical operations and transportation in France for the AEF. Courtesy of Cushing Memorial Library & Archives, Texas A&M University.

A&M alumnus and former chairman of the Texas A&M Board of Directors, Cushing had become a campus and alumni hero as an A&M College advocate in Texas's turbulent political arena, seeking to protect and grow the college. When the war was declared, Cushing, in his mid-50s, initially was rejected for induction into the US Army's Officer Reserve Corps. He pressed his case with political connections and higher-ups in Washington, and, as a result, in late April 1917, he received a direct commission as a major in the US Army, assigned to the 17th Engineer Regiment that was being activated in Atlanta, Georgia. By August 1917, Cushing had landed in France to serve as the director of logistics and debarkation at the strategic ports of Antwerp and Brussels. In early 1918, he was promoted to colonel and took command as the chief AEF transportation officer, with the additional duties of overseeing Mediterranean supply ports and depots. Concerned with adding vital rail and infrastructure, he pushed for the completion of critical bridges, succeeding in what seemed a very short time, and "when the French officers complimented him on his achievement in record time he responded: 'That's nothing, That's the way we do things in Texas.'"[17]

Once mobilized, the biggest challenge was to train and equip the army. While procedures and processes regarding the demands of fielding and supplying army ground forces were generally in place dating back to the Civil War, there was no such template for the emerging US Army Air Service because there had never before been aeroplanes! The early civilian and military pioneers of aviation in general, and military aviation in particular, faced seemingly insurmountable hurdles to put men and "machines" (as aeroplanes were commonly called) in the air. These efforts throughout the war were further complicated by the fact that the Allied air forces and the combatant German air forces were years ahead of American aviation in all respects, including having available pilots, training procedures, combat operations, logistics, and, most critically, credible, well-designed, and tested airplanes to match the enemy. Except for America's ability to quickly recruit aviation cadets and thus potential pilots, all other aspects of the US Army and Navy air services remained profoundly behind the curve.[18]

3

TRAINING
Wooden Sky Coffins

Everyone talked of flying. There was a hitch. They flew—that was right; they flew in machines heavier than air. But they smashed. Sometimes they smashed the engine, sometimes they smashed the aeronaut, usually they smashed both.

—H. G. Wells
The War in the Air
1907

There are only two ways left now of winning the war, and they both begin with 'A'—one is aeroplanes and the other is America.

—Winston Churchill
Munitions Ministers, Great Britain
September 1917

A new era of technology and adventure emerged following the flights of the Wright brothers. Other than a casual sighting of one of a few "aeroplanes," most Americans, aside from a few aspiring pilots and crew members, had little knowledge of flight. The US Army Air Service in its formative days was little more than novelty attached as a department of the Signal Corps. Balloons with gondolas, first used by the Union Army in the July 1862 Peninsula Campaign, had more visibility and appeal than aeroplanes. H. G. Well's 1907 syndicated, fictional story of flight and "aeronauts," *The War in the Air*, further captured the public's imagination. Gradually, prior to 1910, the Wright brothers provided personnel instruction and "licensed" the first dozen US military officers who volunteered for flight training. By 1916, these early American aviators—only a few of whom had any flight experience, which was very limited and in Mexico—were the first to be active in the air service, assisting in the early planning in hopes of wider acceptance of the aeroplane in a military role. Political opposition to all military expansion and the shortage of appropriations prior to 1915 placed the army in general, and the air service in particular,

Table 2. British war office and aviation: five tests for machines of private design Performance Required from Various Military Types (February 1914)

	Range	Crew	Speed	Time to Climb to 3,500 Feet
Light Scout*	300 miles	Pilot only	50–85 mph	5 minutes
Reconnaissance Aeroplane (a)	300 miles	Pilot and observer, and 80 pounds of equipment	45–75 mph	7 minutes
Reconnaissance Aeroplane (b)**	200 miles	Pilot and observer, and equipment	35–60 mph	10 minutes
Fighting*** Aeroplane (a)	200 miles	Pilot and gunner, and 300 pounds of guns and ammunition	45–65 mph	10 minutes
Fighting*** Aeroplane (b)	300	Pilot and gunner, and 100 pounds of equipment	45–75 mph	8 minutes

Miscellaneous qualities: For purposes of calculations, weights of the pilot and passenger are 160 pounds each.
*Capable of being started by pilot single-handedly.
**Able to land over a 30-foot vertical obstacle and pull up within a distance of 100 yards.
*** A clear field of fire in every direction up to 30 degrees from the line of flight.
Note: Instructional aeroplane with an endurance of 150 miles will also be tested under special conditions; safety and ease of handling will be of first importance in this type.

as a very low priority. As European nations made rapid advancements in aviation, America languished. Public notices in British scientific publications routinely read in New York and Washington, DC, as early as 1914, which called for "advanced" aircraft design and performance, seemed to make no impression on American policymakers.[1] See Table 2.

Even after a year of European war following August 1914, the US military received little attention. The army had no vision and President Wilson and Congress had no will to act, instead espousing a policy of "neutrality" based on the country's "two-ocean" isolation. Sea power prior to 1917 was considered the bulwark of American military might and defense. The army thus made plans to advocate for preparedness. One young officer, Lt. Hap Arnold, was assigned to draft a detailed, written study for Congressional presentation on the state of army aviation relative to countries worldwide. America was not even ranked in the top 20 in any category and ranked particularly low in appropriations. Young, vocal officers and aviation pioneers like Arnold, Billy Mitchell, Benjamin Foulois, Birdsey Lewis, and Raynal Bolling were deemed out of place in their advocacy for attention and funding for the air service. After spirited testimony that "shamed the isolationist Congress" into reality, the air service (at a time when the Germans allocated $45 million; Russia, $22 million; Austria, $3 million; and Great Britain,

Figure 11. Aircraft were soon specialized as with the case of the French Voisin III two-seat bomber. Top speed 65 mph, with Hispano-Suiza engines. Courtesy of Wilson Collection.

$1.1 million) was allocated $300,000 in March 1915. The funding was sufficient only to maintain an already poor air fleet and to purchase parts and a few new airplanes.[2]

The next appropriation did not come until mid-1917. By this time, America, the nation in which the Wright brothers pioneered flight, was some five years behind the combatant European nations that had made major strides in advancing all aspects of aviation: design enhancements, endurance records, and combat tactics. In the years prior to the war, the British, French, and Germans made major strides in aeroplane design, manufacture, and utility. These advances were, according to *The Aviation Pocket Book*, published in London in 1917, "enveloped in an atmosphere of secrecy." The Wright brothers, who continued in private to improve their aeroplane, twice asked to provide the US Army with their latest aviation advancements and were twice rejected as "just two more dreamers seeking government funding."

The bad publicity and Congressional protest following Langley's Aerodrome experiments (which were funded with $50,000 from the army), and crashes into the Potomac River, reduced support for the Wrights. In response, prior to the war, the Wrights actively pursued business relationships in Europe and established the world's first commercial aerial training schools in France, Germany, and Italy. Aviation technology developed in America was routinely passed to the British, who as early as 1914 set performance standards for new planes. In contrast, however, the export of advancements in aviation—many the result of innovations inspired and developed by the Wright brothers—as well as data and aeronautic publications from England to America, were marked confidential by the British government's Press Bureau, censored and deemed "forbidden" for circulation.[3]

America's approach to the air service lagged behind Europe's. As soon as President Wilson and Congress committed armed forces, the War Department in Washington panicked in its efforts to address the Allies' requests for thousands of pilots and combat aircraft. When World War I began, the US Air Service had only 23 planes, compared with Germany's 232, France's 162, and Great Britain's 113. Lucian Thayer, in *America's First Eagles*, captures the bleak nature of the US Army Air Service:

> One squadron, equipped with obsolete airplanes;
>
> No machines fit for front-line service;

No aero accessory equipment of any type;

No fundamental knowledge of air operations;

Fewer than fifty trained pilots;

No pilot, save those serving with the French army, who was capable of performing a battle mission;

Only five officers in Europe, none of whom had yet acquired an advanced technical knowledge;

This was the equipment with which the United States, in April 1917, faced a war in the air.[4]

The roots of the US Air Service and the advancement of American military aviation were founded in the response to the war and technology by the British and the French to the advances of the German air force.[5] Given the war clouds of early 1914, the nations of Europe expanded their militaries as America watched and waited. While trench warfare on the Western Front soon reached a near stalemate, the aviation sector made major strides in technology and strategy, having significant impact on the war's outcome. And thus the conclusions reached by Winston Churchill in

Figure 12. The war produced numerous experimental aircraft in search of improved planes. Pictured here is the French Caudron G-4, crew of two with a maximum speed of 80 mph, LeRhone rotary engines, and a ceiling of 14,000 feet. The high-drag pusher configuration limited performance. Courtesy of Wilson Collection.

1917 for American airpower, followed by months of deadly stalemate and horrific carnage, set the stage for America's entry in the war.[6]

As the war progressed between late 1914 and early 1917, the US Air Service worked to establish its existence and relevance with the available machines and personnel. Early US flight training for both the army and the navy was a daily work in progress. Given that there was virtually no commercial-civilian aviation or airline industry across the country from which to draw, finding pilots, ground crews, and mechanics, and developing methods for training them, remained a tremendous challenge. As early aviator and air service pioneer Lt. Henry H. "Hap" Arnold recalled, "No flight was routine." Prior to 1917, there was no organized ground school, no ground or flight check lists, no control towers, no weather reports, no navigation aids (or even maps), no mention of flight safety, no reliable engines or high-quality fuel. Pilots were trained to make "dead-stick" landings on the assumption they would not fly long before they experienced engine failure. Goggles were introduced only after pilots sustained eye injuries while flying in open-cockpit aircraft. Early airplanes had no fuel gauges, leading one pilot to comment that his "clock," or watch, was the most important instrument because it was "my fuel gauge." Capt. Ben Foulois, who learned to fly in the "'bucking' abilities [of the Model B Wright Flyer] in gusty Texas winds," recalled in early 1950 that, "we had no parachutes in those days—headquarters had declared them 'defeatist'—and we were instructed to 'stick with the ship.' So, in order to stick to the ship thereafter, I used a four-foot trunk strap with which I lashed myself to the pilot's seat—in other words, the initial 'safety belt' used in the US Air Force."[7]

The essence of the pending departure of thousands of troops, sailors, and aviators eager to fulfill their patriotic duty, and the unknown challenges awaiting them, was vividly expressed by Texas A&M aviation cadet Harry B. Moses '18 in a letter home to Burnet, Texas, just before departing to Europe:

> This morning I am packing and suppose I shall be on my way. This is my last letter until I get on the other side but I shall write you as often as I can "over there."
>
> As I wrote Dad, I don't know when I shall get back or whether I shall get back. I shall certainly be glad when my train rolls [back] into Burnet but if I don't I shall only be one of the many who have died in this just cause.

I leave without fear of my fate or its consequences. If it is willed that I shall not come back I am willing to bow to that will but the German who brings me down is going to have to fight like Hell and I only hope I shall be able to give them some hot lead myself. There is nothing I would like better than return to my home and friends with medals on my breast or a record. I want to come back whole or not at all. I don't want to come back minus a leg or arm or eye or any part of my body. That is one reason I like the aviation. A man comes back whole or he doesn't come back.[8]

Good luck and God bless you . . . everyone
Lovingly your son,
Harry

The Right Stuff

New pilots had to be skilled and fearless, with thorough knowledge of engine mechanics. Planes built of spruce, glued fabric, and wires crashed daily as pilots took off and landed on unfamiliar fields and maneuvered over and around obstacles. In addition to the extensive army and navy specialty training programs in mechanics, radio maintenance, and meteorology at Texas A&M, the War Department rushed to mobilize aviation

Figure 13. While looking for the "Right Stuff" among new young pilots, crash landings both in training and on the battlefront were a routine event. Here an American Curtiss JN4, the primary training aircraft, would become a barn-storming favorite during the postwar 1920s. Courtesy of Wilson Collection.

schools at six educational institutions around the country. Trainees who finished introductory training at Texas A&M, as well as newly commissioned officers from Camp Funston in Kansas, were referred to begin flight training. Rushed into service on April 6, 1917, at six different institutions, the same week that Camp Funston opened, the first flight classes numbered 25 cadet trainees, and each program was expected to graduate 200 certified pilots every three months.[9]

Six flight preparatory schools, or Schools of Military Aeronautics (SMAs), were established to provide ground school instruction in motor mechanics, topography, wireless telegraphy, photography, and the principles of flight. They were placed at the University of California at Berkeley, Ohio University in Columbus, University of Illinois at Urbana, University of Texas at Austin, Massachusetts Institute of Technology in Boston, and Cornell University in Ithaca, New York. These eight-week flight ground schools were only a small supplement to formal military aviation training, which tended to concentrate on limited advanced training and tactics. A shortage of instructors and aircraft limited enhanced instruction until late 1918.[10]

Generally, those in the Army Air Service or Naval Air Service after mid-1917, regardless if they were a pilot, observer, mechanic, or ground crew member, took "engineering" courses at one of the six institutions prior to departing for Europe or being assigned in the United States for flight training or logistical support. Those who had already departed to the American Expeditionary Force (AEF) or missed the ground school took comparable courses in Great Britain, France, or Italy. A very few Americans, such as Ensign Jesse Easterwood '09, Lt. Guy Adriance '15, and Lt. Henry A. Armstrong '18, attended aviation engineering programs in England and Italy as part of their precheck qualifications to ferry Italian planes to France.

Training for air service personnel was broken into a number of categories and functions: entry-level aviation cadets and pilots, observers and gunners, mechanics and engineers, and logistical support. Pilot training in mid-1917 was only a general overview and introduction to the basics of flight. Cadets had six to eight weeks to qualify for their "wings." The initial War Department plan was to train newly commissioned, college-educated officer candidates as lieutenants, yet by April 1918, aviation demand dictated that potential pilots would be inducted as "aviation cadets" to expedite screening and qualification of pilot trainees. Those who survived were commissioned and sent to France. Until 1918, advanced pilot training on formation flying, tactics, and bombing was conducted overseas, where instructors with more experience, including combat experience, and much more advanced, combat-ready aircraft were located.[11] In an interview with the *Temple* [Texas] *Daily Telegram*, Maj. Clinton W. Russell '12, commanding officer of the Air Service pilot training school at Rich Field, Waco, provided a detailed "explanatory statement" on aviation qualifications and the high expectations surrounding pilot selection and training:

> Only the very best in American manhood is good enough for the aviation section and only the best men available will be taken [for training]. We must have a high type of man for this work because there is a high type of work for him to do. He must be intelligent, because only an intelligent man can grasp the full significance of the trust and confidence reposed in him. He must be a true American.
>
> I want every man who applies first to consider carefully what he is going to do, to weigh himself in the balance and make certain that he will not be found wanting. After he has been tried out by experts and found to be *the right stuff*, I want him to know that he will be well taken care of, that he will be in a red-blooded, thoroughly trained and excellently equipped fighting branch, and that he will be proud to be serving in the aviation section.[12]

Thus, the heart of the challenge of complementing the military preflight programs was to ramp up flight training fields across the country to screen, process, and qualify pilots. A majority of the training fields were in the Southwest due to winter weather conditions that limited flying north of the Mason-Dixon line. Influenced by the Wright Brothers and political pressure from Washington, a few advanced training bases opened in Ohio and New York (despite weather limitations), but the bulk of aviation instruction was in Texas. Eleven airfields in Texas were fully operational in the spring of 1918, representing 40 percent of all training fields and producing over 65 percent of all pilots, observers, and gunners. The process involved both newly commissioned officers and cadets, who became the majority of those processed to both increase the number of trained airmen and to allow for an assessment of those to be advanced for further training either in the United States or, once they arrived in AEF, in France or England. The first screening was an introductory ground school course such as the School of Military Aeronautics, with limited screening at the San

Antonio Aviation Center (renamed Kelly Field). Other primary aviation fields in Texas included Love Field in Dallas, Carruthers Field in Benbrook, Hicks Field northwest of Fort Worth, and Barron Field in Everman. Southern locations that processed the largest number of Texas Aggie aviators and crews included Post Field, Fort Still, Oklahoma; Payne Field, West Point, Mississippi; Gerstner Field, Lake Charles, Louisiana; and the balloon-observation school at Omaha, Nebraska.[13] See Table 3.

Trained aviation mechanics were in short supply throughout the war. The air service concentrated a majority of the mechanical and engine training at Texas A&M; St. Paul, Minnesota; Kelly Field, San Antonio; and Scott Field, Illinois.

Table 3. Texas Army Air Service flight training fields, 1917–1919

Field	Location	Function	Maximum Number of Cadets
Barron*	Everman	Primary training	300
Brooks	San Antonio	Instructor training	300
Call	Wichita Falls	Observer training	300
Carruthers*	Benbrook	Primary training	300
Ellington**	Houston	Bombing school	600
Kelly	San Antonio	Primary training	600
Ream (Park Place)	Houston	Primary training	200
Love	Dallas	Primary training	300
Rich	Waco	Primary training	300
Hicks*	Fort Worth	Aerial gunnery	180
Camp Dick	Dallas	Cadet gunner	4,500
NAS	Galveston	*Under construction Oct. 1918	

* Hicks, Barron, and Carruthers Fields were considered part of the "Taliaferro" training area, which included other auxiliary fields near Lake Worth.
**Early Air Service fields were named for aviators killed in military training crashes in 1913–1914 and included Hugh Kelly, Moss L. Love, Rex Chandler, Joseph D. Park, Erie Ellington, W. R. Talliaferro, and Henry Post.

Airplane silhouettes (relative sizes) illustrating representative British, French, Italian, American, and German planes—some that were used for the first time during World War I—to help airmen and troops on the ground distinguish between friendly or enemy aircraft. Author's collection.

To address the growing demand for aircraft techs, hundreds of ground personnel were trained in British and French aircraft factories. By April 1918, the US Army and Navy established advanced training camps in France, at Tours and Issoudun. Trained American flight instructors with combat experience, as well as improved aircraft, parts, fuel, and trained mechanics and ground crews, were slow in arriving, however. Pilots joked about the "wooden crates" they flew, yet seemed encouraged when US manufacturers began to ship American-made planes. The first to arrive in France was the De Havilland DH-4, on May 14, 1918. The new DH-4, designed to fly at 130 miles per hour and obtain an altitude of 10,000 feet in 10 minutes, fully loaded, received mixed reviews from crews in the AEF, with the army inspector general declaring in *The New York Times* that the "machines compare favorably with the best British and French makes." Pilots in the air over France, however, dubbed them "flying coffins" due to the pressurized, highly flammable gas tank placed between the pilot and observer, which resulted in horrific losses of crews.[14]

No effective, heavy bomber was designed or built during the war. The bulky British Handley-Page and the Italian Caproni bombers, with their

Figure 15. The British-designed Handley-Page heavy bomber was the first aircraft to conduct strategic bombing missions. Flown by a crew of three, the bomber had a range of 450 miles, top speed of 98 mph, and a ceiling of 8,500 feet. The 13,000-pound aircraft, when loaded with eight 250-pound bombs, had a rate of climb of 217 feet per minute. Courtesy of Wilson Collection.

underpowered Fiat engines and leaking gas tanks, proved to be just as inferior and dangerous. While these bombers carried out a number of successful bombing raids, the Allied pilot death rate due to accidents, poor construction, and vulnerability over enemy targets far exceeded their airworthiness.

At home, a different type of death would send the nation into near panic and substantially halt military operations and training, as well as impact civilians across the nation and the world, just as General Pershing's army launched the biggest Western Front counteroffensive of the war. As newspaper headlines across the nation carried reports of the battles and casualties on the Western Front, speculation grew that a truce or peace would be in place by Christmas 1918. In the meantime, an influenza pandemic swept the country, with headlines reporting widespread death. The full extent of this influenza pandemic has never been understood or documented.

The October 1918 Terror

The training of thousands of troops nationwide resulted in the greatest mobilization the nation had ever known. Support personnel and material, such as the medical service, medical supplies, hospital availability, and emergency equipment, could not keep pace with screening, training, and healthcare needs. The most crippling event would be an uncontrollable influenza epidemic to which there was no full ability to respond. Such an epidemic would directly impact the preparation and training of troops in the homeland, as well as the ability to support troops in the AEF. Any doubt that this global event would affect health and safety at the local level was replaced with near panic as the so-called Spanish influenza swept across America in the fall of 1918.[15]

Reports of a deadly outbreak of influenza in Boston that spread to Philadelphia and across the nation soon had a direct impact on army cantonments (or bases) in general, and in particular on the Texas A&M campus and surrounding region. The original location of the 1918 epidemic has been debated for about a century, with no conclusion other than that the illness moved rapidly beginning in mid-August 1918 along the Atlantic coast and spreading westward and southward. Rumors and anecdotal reports of influenza were replaced with detailed stories (including daily death tolls) in newspapers across the nation. In the South, the influenza gained entry via coastal areas and port cities, then spread rapidly. In San Antonio, for example, over half of the population, some 80,000 citizens, became ill, affecting every household. In Houston, the epidemic went grossly underreported, with dozens dying every day, leading to a coffin shortage. Texas A&M President Bizzell, the A&M staff, and Brazos County leaders were well aware of the threat, given the large number of transient military personnel on the campus from across the country. On September 29, 1918, President Bizzell placed the campus under mandatory quarantine. This was the first such sweeping action since October 1897, when A&M College President Lawrence S. Ross and Mayor Adams of Bryan placed the campus and city under a strict quarantine, ordering that no trains were to stop either in the city or at the campus until the threatening epidemic sweeping South Texas was under control. The quarantine was "deemed advisable by reason of the development of 'grippe,'" the name generally used during this period for the deadly influenza-pneumonia illness.[16]

President Bizzell issued strict orders that all A&M cadets, staff, and soldiers in training would not leave or return to the college via trains or automobiles, "thus subjecting themselves to the likelihood of catching cold [influenza] which might in turn develop grippe." He stated that doctors were available and that arrangements had been made to acquire additional nurses in order to give patients the best possible care. This, in fact, was an exaggeration. He concluded: "This statement is made to allay any fear that may have arisen as a result of wild rumors over the situation." Bizzell and army personnel knew from communications with camps around the country that the situation was not mere rumor but a looming emergency. Bizzell instructed A&M Commandant of the Corps of Cadets, Major Fred W. Zeller, to place the campus "under guard," with armed sentinels "at all entrances to the campus" and to "keep someone there day and night, with other sentinels . . . placed at important points on the campus during special hours [such as the arrival and departure of trains] of the day and night." When asked by the *Bryan Daily Eagle* about the use of armed sentinels, Bizzell said this was to protect construction materials intended for new buildings and "to prevent automobile drivers from driving on thee lawns." In fact, there was no problem with the construction materials and the "lawns" were not the problem![17]

It was hoped that the unseasonably warm early October weather, accentuated by a four-month drought, would lower the likelihood of an epidemic. Within days, however, severe cases of influenza spread on the A&M campus and into the local community. Additional military medical

personnel were sent from San Antonio and the order for quarantine rein-
stated and monitored. All campus gatherings and activities in Bryan, such
as sporting events, dances, movies, and church services, were cancelled
until further notice. There was to be no travel to out-of-town football
games until after mid-November, and then only two trips were permit-
ted, with the traveling teams "not to remain away longer than forty-eight
hours on each trip." Texas A&M Coach D. V. "Tubby" Graves reported that
a great many players on the football team were bedridden with the flu,
but there were no deaths. Reports from across the nation soon reached
the campus. Overwhelmed, the army briefly delayed the draft inductions
scheduled nationwide. Army training at the college was curtailed only
briefly given the pressure on the staff to produce trained troops as quickly
as possible. All incoming military flights of equipment and support staff
were grounded until further notice. And then, the influenza epidemic hit
the A&M campus.[18]

By late September, more than two dozen cadets and Army trainees were
patients in the small, campus hospital, and less than week later, hundreds
across campus fell ill. Hospital staffing across the nation was taxed to the
maximum as the army demanded more doctors and nurses in Europe to
care for the rising number of wounded Americans. With more than 2 million US troops in France alone, and more scheduled to be deployed, the
call was for "one thousand nurses a week" for the next eight weeks, re-
ducing the supply of nurses in civilian hospitals at home. Brazos County
officials quickly recognized the magnitude of the outbreak. Campus staff
members were assisted by the American Red Cross and volunteer women's
auxiliaries in Bryan, College, and Kurten to care for and comfort the sick.
The cause of the first reported death on campus, cadet F. J. Butschek of
Moulton, Texas, on October 1, 1918, was determined to be pneumonia.
The spread of the illness was overpowering. Symptoms that could develop
in a matter of hours terrified otherwise healthy troops, faculty, and cadets:
blood pouring from the nose, ears, and eye sockets; inflamed throats; vom-
iting; fever; extreme headaches; and in some cases, agonizing delirium.
The death toll continued to climb during early October.[19]

Medical staff and local volunteers at the college could do very little other than attempt to make patients comfortable, and, to the extent possible,
limit the spread of the disease. Despite the high incidence of illness in
San Antonio, the army sent additional doctors and nurses from Fort Sam
Houston to Texas A&M. The campus hospital was overwhelmed. Between

Table 4. Spanish influenza deaths: A&M College of Texas, October 1918

Name	Date of death	Hometown	Status
F.J. Butschek	Oct 1, 1918	Moulton	cadet
Roland M. Davis	Oct 4, 1918	Gary, OK	army
Ord F. Strickler	Oct 6, 1918	Houston	army
Sam H. Harmonson	Oct 7, 1918	Archer City	army
Albert J. Holz	Oct 8, 1918	Lahoma, OK	army
August J. Saunders	Oct 8, 1918	Navasota	army
Irvin A. Carroll	Oct 9, 1918	Sabine Pass	army
Clara Bell Hollyfield	Oct 9, 1918	Waco	civilian nurse
Harold G. Maia	Oct 9, 1918	Stillwater, OK	army
Theodore Metzger	Oct 9, 1918	Galveston	army
Alvin A. Anderson	Oct 10, 1918	Stoughton, MO	army
William A. Childress	Oct 10, 1918	Muskogee, OK	army
Jesse H. Engle	Oct 10, 1918	Francisville, IL	army
Wallace C. Kilker	Oct 10, 1918	Lemar, IA	army
John J. McAtee	Oct 10, 1918	Goteba, OK	army
George E. Buchanan	Oct 11, 1918	Chickasha, OK	army
Robert W. Clayton	Oct 11, 1918	Austin	army
Hubert H. Hill	Oct 11, 1918	Lufkin	cadet
Harvey L. Johnson	Oct 11, 1918	Graham	cadet
Edward A. Murray	Oct 11, 1918	Coalburg, WV	army
James E. Reed	Oct 12, 1918	Camp, WV	army
Homer Rush	Oct 12, 1918	Pryor, OK	army
John E. Webb 'x 18	Oct 13, 1918	Bryan	former cadet
Peter H. Agropian	Oct 13, 1918	Brookshire	cadet
Doyle G. Brooks	Oct 13, 1918	Frost	cadet
Vincent M. Robertson	Oct 13, 1918	Beaumont	cadet
G. Leigh Jones	Oct 13, 1918	San Juan	army
Virgil M. Marshall	Oct 13, 1918	Cordell, OK	army

Name	Date of death	Hometown	Status
John E. Anderson	Oct 14, 1918	Boone, IA	army
Joseph M. Nance	Oct 14, 1918	Gaymond, OK	army
Joseph R. Power	Oct 14, 1918	Level, WV	army
Mrs. Victor Marshall	Oct 14, 1918	Cordell, OK	soldier's wife
Prof. I.R. Barwls'10	Oct 15, 1918	Childress	radio instructor
Rife J. Hopkins	Oct 16, 1918	McCurtain, OK	army
Thomas W. Rambold	Oct 16, 1918	Junction	cadet
Claude H. Smith	Oct 16, 1918	Carnago, OK	army
Leslie D. Alford	Oct 17, 1918	Okmulgee, OK	army
Edward D. Klaedner	Oct 18, 1918	San Antonio	army
C. Fred Beauchamp	Oct 19, 1918	Orange	cadet
James H. Eagle	Oct 19, 1918	Indianapolis, IN	army
Arthur W. Zappe	Oct 22, 1918	Ballinger	cadet
Bradford P. Day	Oct 23, 1918		A&M College Bandmaster*
Issac L. Maxwell	Oct 23,1918	Coryell, CO	army
Mrs. Lynn W. Friley	Oct 24, 1918		wife of A&M College

Registrar Source: Bill Page, *When Aggieland Turned Khaki: World War I at Texas A&M*, July 25, 2016; Bryan Daily Eagle, Oct 1918; Texas A&M Alumni Quarterly, 1918.
*B.P. Day had been director of the A&M College since 1904.

October 4 and 11, some 20 army trainees died on campus. Local residents were terrified that, despite scattered civilian deaths around the county, the disease would spread to kill even more. Local elected officials in Bryan and a citizens group, formerly known as the Brazos Defense Council, telegraphed the War Department with their concerns about local conditions and demanded additional assistance.[20] As the hospital exceeded capacity, barracks became sick wards. Charles Crawford '19, then a cadet at A&M, recalled the experience:

> At that time there were two wooden army barracks. There were students in those, enlisted men both upstairs and down, and at times there were so many of those fellows who had flu and were deathly ill that there weren't enough up running around to even wait on them. We had as many as five or six of those fellows dying a night. The local undertaking establishment couldn't keep enough caskets to bury them in, and they would come out with these long wicker baskets about six feet long shaped like the old Egyptian mummies. The hospital was full and running over. They say some people had a walking case, and that's what I had. I've never seen such a horrible nasal discharge as there were from the men who had the flu, and of course, much of it went into pneumonia and that's what caused many deaths.[21]

Figure 16. Charles W. Crawford '19 (left) was an eyewitness to the massive October 1918 influenza outbreak and death on the A&M campus. He joined the faculty in 1921 and retired as professor emeritus of mechanical engineering in 1965. He is the author of *One Hundred Years of Engineering at Texas A&M* (1976). Courtesy of Cushing Memorial Library & Archives, Texas A&M University.

In response to the concerns of Bryan citizens, A&M officials were aggressive in requesting assistance in advance of and during the pandemic, which overwhelmed all available resources. As early as April 1918, President Bizzell, in anticipation of the influx of trainees, contacted the army to request immediate funding to build a hospital on the campus adequate for the growing number of troops, staff, and their families. The army's response was delayed into the fall, when Bizzell went to Washington, DC, and secured $55,000 to build a new hospital—too late to assist with the outbreak in October. Anxiety on campus escalated following the deaths on October 23 of Lynn Friley, wife of the college registrar, and B. Pierre Day, the popular director of the Texas Aggie Band. As the death toll increased so, too, did the apprehension of troops, cadets, staff, and families about what appeared to be a lack of proper care for the sick.[22]

At the height of the national epidemic, US forces under General Pershing and allies on the Western Front engaged in one of the largest ground offensives, along the St. Mihiel salient. A sector of the front acquired from the bloodied and demoralized French army was pulled from the trenches and reassigned to American forces. The Allied plan was to push the entrenched Germans back as quickly as possible to the railhead at Mat-la Tour and Conflans. Combat casualty reports from the front were reported in newspapers across the country daily and generally overshadowed stories of the influenza epidemic. These reports were further embellished by wild rumors that a truce was in the works. President Wilson, along with French and British spokesmen, was quoted daily on a range of peace talk possibilities. Meanwhile, by late October, some 250,000 American troops per week were preparing to move to East Coast embarkation ports for transport to France. The draft was increased to acquire and train more troops for follow-on offenses being planned—if the war continued—for early 1919. In the Dallas area, the newly organized 10th Regiment of Infantry comprising Texas A&M former students was quickly making final plans to fill its ranks and train for shipment to France in December 1918. The regiment included many notable Texas Aggies not already in uniform and was commanded by Col. Abe Ross of Waco, with a staff of eight officers, including notables Lt. Col. Marion S. Church, Capt. Glenn L. Sneed (one of the era's best-known evangelists), and a machine gun company led by Capt. L. J. Smith of Amarillo. The unit, expected to number 1,000, 200 at full strength, had three battalions, commanded by first battalion, Maj. Joe Utay '08 of Dallas, second battalion, Maj. John D. McCall of Austin, and third battalion, Maj. Richard H. Standifer of Fort Worth.[23]

By September 25, the flu epidemic was clearly engulfing New York City, Boston, Philadelphia, Cleveland, and Atlanta, killing more than 100 people per day. While newspapers noted the growing epidemic, they offered only meager information. A. A. Hoehling, in the *Great Epidemic* (1961), described the response by civic leaders: "There was, apparently, a tacit conspiracy among the nation's editors to hush-hush the ever-mounting ravages, as though they hoped that if they were not noticed, the infection would go away." The so-called infection and spreading epidemic did not go away.[24]

The great irony of the 1918 influenza epidemic is that more Americans died at its height—over 45,000 in October alone—than did American troops through hostile actions on the Western Front (7,547). From October 5 to 26, 10,958 deaths were reported in Philadelphia alone, along with more than 10,000 deaths across Texas and 51 deaths of cadets, army trainees, families, and staff on the Texas A&M campus. In most cities and army camps in Texas, the epidemic started near the end of September. The first cases generally ran six to eight weeks in rural areas and three to four weeks in the cramped cities and army camps with crowded barracks and poor medical treatment. Hospitals and medical staff were overwhelmed. There was no known cure.[25]

While the deaths on the A&M campus and across Texas resulted in local coverage and concern, the news media and army officials seemed to focus exclusively on the war. The epidemic struck just as the nation was at its most critical stage of training troops and transporting troops and supplies to Europe. By early November 1918, military demands and the war bond drive across Texas and the nation overshadowed the dark, deadly days of the previous month's pandemic.

And before long, rumors of an armistice overshadowed everything else.

OVER THERE
Hun in the Sun

Our air service will take the offensive to all points with the object of destroying the enemy's air service, attacking his troops on the ground and protecting our own air and ground troops.

—William "Billy" Mitchell
September 11, 1918

It's all very true war isn't what it's cracked up to be. Lots of times you have a longing for quiet pastures when the odds loom up against you. Personally, I had rather die a dozen times than to have folks say I didn't do my duty.

—Lt. Mitchell H. Brown '16

Few Texans of the era had ever been more than a couple of hundred miles from home, and far fewer had ventured to another state. This would change quickly for A&M students—and former students who entered active military duty and trained at camps, airfields, and civilian institutions across the nation. The ocean voyage from New York City or Hoboken, New Jersey, to the war in Europe would have been even more of an eye-opener.

A story about Aggie aviator Lt. Walter Wotipka 'x17, from Victoria, paints a vivid picture of his voyage and arrival for duty in France:

> One day some names were posted on the bulletin board [at Texas A&M] with orders stating that these people would proceed to Leon Springs for training. While there he heard of a need for aviators so he requested a transfer. He was sent to the University of Texas where he studied navigation and meteorology. After six weeks of ground school he was sent to North Island near San Diego, California, where he started flight training in the "Flying Jennies." They were based on an island so that a speedboat could pick up those flyers unfortunate to fall into the water. Wotipka spent six months there, then sent for more training in Louisiana and on to Hoboken, N.J., for two weeks before he boarded a ship for overseas.
>
> Three to four hundred died of the flu on the way over and after a very rough and hard voyage they arrived in Liverpool, England. The harbor was so shallow the boat was placed in a lock in order to unload. After three days in Liverpool they started across the channel with a boatload of horses. The water was so rough that many lockers and other equipment was washed overboard. Halfway over they had a breakdown and the boat stopped in mid-channel. After many anxious hours, they got it going again. Of course, German submarines were always in the channel.
>
> Wotipka reported to an airfield at Issoudun, near Orleans, about 120 miles south of Paris. There he was assigned as a flight instructor and started teaching other pilots. They were flying the Italian Spads with a V-8 motor and French Nieuports with rotary engines. He and the pilots were part of the US Signal Corps and the old time Army men considered the [training] aircraft of dubious value. Much of the time on both sides of the war was spent shooting down each other's observation balloons. The planes had little effect on ground action.
>
> There were no control towers or radar, so flag men were used on the ground to control takeoffs and landings. Vickers machine guns were timed to shoot through the revolving propellers. The pilots would steal cook stove lids from the kitchen and place them under their [wicker] seats [in the plane], hoping to deflect some of the ground fire which always came their way.

Wotipka, who the *Victoria Advocate* called "One of the daring young men of the wild blue yonder," was promoted to captain and served in France until May 1919. Like many of the returning veterans he did not return to finish his degree, instead opting to go in business and opened a Ford dealership in Waelder, Texas.[1]

The first Americans to arrive in Britain with an interest in flying were processed by the army and assigned to the Royal Air Force (RAF) for evaluation, which was not intensive given the demand for pilots and crew. While the British and French had significantly improved aviation by the fall of 1914 and early 1915, flight operations were still in their infancy. New flight cadets studied at what would become known as ground school and took an orientation flight almost from their first day on the "field." After this briefest of introductions, many pilots became self-taught, flying solo mere hours after their "instruction." When this training in England ended, pilots were sent to either France or Italy. During the war's early months, pilots tossed small bombs over the side of their open-air cockpits by hand and carried handguns and rifles for protection. Once on the frontlines, the average life expectancy of a pilot, most of whom had less than 24 hours of flight time, was about three weeks.[2]

In France, airmen and their crews were moved from field to field for additional training. The shortage of aircraft and experienced instructors delayed the ability to meet the scheduled demand for pilots. Henry Moses, still an aviation cadet without rank, was among those delayed. To fill the time, crews formed camp football and baseball teams and wrote letters home. Henry remained in touch with his family by weekly mail. Concerned with the cost of his brother Tad's expenses at the A&M College, he arranged with the paymaster to send $15 of his $35 monthly pay directly to the campus. Following introductory flight training in France, Moses was sent to Camp Ovesto at Foggia, Italy, to complete his training and earn his wings, along with his officer's commission. In a letter home, he said he was pleased to be in "sunny Italy" rather than the damp, dark, and crowded barracks in France: "I have a single bed and even have a pillow" he noted. After Italy, he was transferred back to Tours, France, for more advanced training in the Nieuport bi-plane.[3]

The increasing number of American troops sent to the AEF created massive logistical problems that gradually flowed down to the troops. Troops were allowed to write letters only—no postal cards—and eventually could no longer receive packages from home without approval from a commanding officer. The rules became so confusing and convoluted that Lieutenant Moses and his friends pulled strings to get basic items

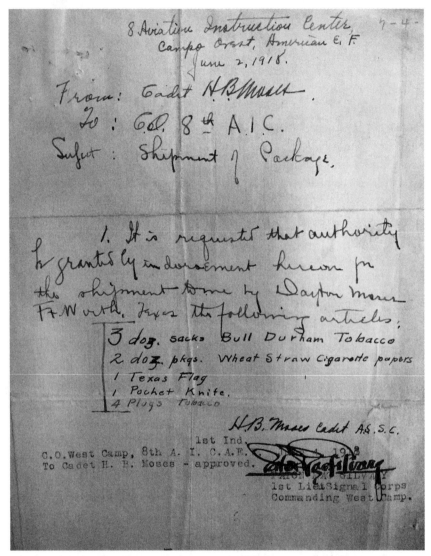

Figure 17. Request by Lt. Harry Moses to send him a Texas flag along with some articles shipped to him from his home in Burnet to France. By mid-June 1918, the US Army was restricting such "care-packages" due to their weight and shortage of shipping capacity across the Atlantic. Moses appealed and his package was approved. Moses Papers, courtesy of Dolph Briscoe Center for American History, University of Texas at Austin.

such as Bull Durham tobacco and warm clothing—and a Texas flag—
through the growing tangle of red tape. Henry's father, Dayton Moses,
chief legal counsel to the Fort Worth–based Cattle Raisers Association
of Texas, wrote directly to the army adjutant general in Washington to
clear up the delay and allow packages to go to his son and all troops. After
three months, Lieutenant Moses received his package.[4]

Flight Duty

The story of Texas Aggie air crews spans the duration of the war and includes a cross-section of aerial jobs. These pilots began service first in the
British, French, and Italian air forces and, following the April 1917 declaration of war, saw service in all branches of the American armed forces.
Some who flew first in the European air forces later transferred into active American units. The pilots, observers, gunners, and crew members
ranged in rank from private to colonel—but in air combat, such distinc-

Figure 18. Lt. Henry
Ainsworth Armstrong '18,
pictured in November
1917, of the Royal British
Air Corps was among
the early group of cadets
that departed college and
volunteered for service
in the British and French
army. Courtesy of Royal
Aero Club.

tions mattered very little. Following in the footsteps of Captain Jouine, who became a famed tank commander before America entered the war, was Lt. Henry A. Armstrong '18, who left Texas early to join the Royal Air Corps.

Experience (including numerous crash landings and near misses), a cool demeanor, enough savvy to control finicky, often experimental equipment in mid-flight, and luck were among the requirements of those who flew above the Western Front. Following orientation and advanced training with AEF units, pilots were placed into one of three categories: pursuit, observation (and gunners), or bombardment. Opinions varied on the use of military aviation—new to both the battleground and the sky—in combat. In the high command, General Pershing was resigned to use aircraft solely as "support" for ground operations, while French Gen. Ferdinand Foch, a throwback to the Napoleonic era, was adamant that "as an instrument of war, [the airplane] is worthless!" More than 75 of the some 250 Texas A&M former cadets who joined the air service as pilots,

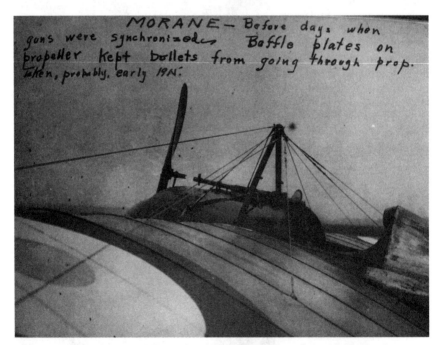

Figure 19. A very unique picture taken by Lt. Harry Moses '18 with the caption: "Before days when guns were synchronized baffle plates on the propeller kept bullets from going through prop. Taken, probably early 1915." Moses Papers, courtesy of Dolph Briscoe Center for American History, University of Texas at Austin.

observers, and crew members were deployed to England, France, and Italy with the AEF. During the course of the war, dozens were decorated for acts of valor. Each had a story to tell.[5]

American pilots with the Royal Air Corps, in cooperation with the US Navy, were rushed into duty to counter the German U-boat threat in the Atlantic. Their daily missions to suppress attacks on allied shipping were complemented by aerial scout planes and a network of observation balloons, the primary assignments of which were to track enemy troops and logistical movements, as well as to direct support for artillery fire. Once the front lines became a labyrinth of trenches and a stalemate was reached, they almost never saw their target and depended on forward air observers to direct fire and report on effectiveness. To accomplish this required Allied pilots to conduct perilous, low-level recon missions. Lee Kennett in *The First Air War, 1914–1918* noted, "The risk of flying—real or imagined—do not seem to have preoccupied the students over much, perhaps because at the age of 20 one's own mortality is not that easy to grasp, but also because the very idea of flying excited them far more than it frightened them."[6]

U-Boat Hunters

The first US air units to fly combat missions in World War I belonged to the navy. Once the British Royal Navy had pinned the German surface fleet in their ports, the primary menace became German submarines. Many of these early operations by naval aviators were anti-submarine patrols seeking to detect German U-boats in the area of Dunkirk off the coast of France. Many airmen had trained with the British and French, and most missions were flown using French aircraft such as Le Tellier flying boats. These planes were slow in speed and slow to climb, subject to poor handling in high wind, and able to carry out only short-range missions. Despite this, the first major organized air operations were conducted by the US Navy to build improved seaplanes with long-range capability. Furthermore, these "observation" missions, often in unarmed aircraft, were some of the war's most important and dangerous. It was in this effort that a number of Texas Aggie aviators excelled.

Shortly after America entered the war, Jesse "Red" Easterwood '09 of Wills Point, Texas, enlisted in the US Navy, qualified for flight training, and was sent to the US Naval Air Station at Pensacola, Florida, for primary training. A member of Company B of the A&M Corps of Cadets,

Figure 20. Lt. Jesse "Red" Easterwood '09 was the first naval aviator from Texas A&M. Trained first at Pensacola, Florida, he was assigned to the Royal Flying Corps to fly the Handley-Page heavy bomber; for his heroic service he was awarded the Navy Cross. Courtesy of Wilson Collection.

he excelled academically and played second base on the college baseball team. After graduating, he settled down in Mexia, Texas, where he ran a small business. This all came to an end in April 1917. At 30 years of age, he was one of the first class of navy cadets to qualify as an aviator and soon was commissioned and awarded his wings. He served briefly as an instructor pilot at Pensacola before transferring to Massachusetts Institute of Technology to complete special courses in engineering.[7]

With few combat aircraft available for training, Ensign Easterwood was ordered to Britain and placed on "loan," first with the Royal Flying Corps (RFC) and then with the French. He was assigned to the RFC No. 214 Squadron to fly into combat the newest aircraft in the war, one of the first 19 British-designed Handley-Page heavy bombers. Advanced flight training by the British included rigorous instruction in gunnery, bombardment, navigation, and night flying. Once qualified, Easterwood flew

Figure 21. A number of American pilots and numerous Texas Aggies were assigned to train and ferry planes from Italy to France. The most popular bomber was the Italian Triplane Caproni Ca-4 bomber. This heavy bomber was under powered until 400 hp L-12 water-cooled American Liberty engines were added. The wood fuselage aircraft had fabric covering and cruised at 90 mph at a ceiling of 10,000 feet. Courtesy of Wilson Collection.

16 missions behind German lines, attacking transportation hubs, supply depots, and troop movements. He flew additional coastal patrol missions to observe enemy movements. As the war progressed, he flew temporarily with both the French and Italian air forces, ferrying the first tri-wing Caproni bomber from Italy to Paris. He ultimately was transferred to an American squadron. For his heroic service, Lieutenant Easterwood was awarded the Navy Cross.[8]

Easterwood remained on active duty as a navy test pilot and instructor. In 1919, he was transferred to the Panama Canal Zone to test new aircraft. On May 16, while facing severe engine trouble on return from a test flight, he attempted an emergency landing and was killed. This popular former student and pioneer aviator was recognized with the naming of the College Station airport near the Texas A&M campus as Jesse L. Easterwood Field on May 22, 1941.

Lt. Jesse L. Easterwood
Pilot, Seaplane Detachment, US Navy Aviation Forces
Date of Action: World War I
Citation: The Navy Cross is awarded to Ensign Jesse L. Easterwood,
US Navy reserve, for distinguished and heroic service as a seaplane
pilot in which capacity he made flights patrolling the sea and bomb-
ing the enemy coasts, showing at all times courage and a high spirit
of duty.

Many men enlisted without pursuing an officer commission, instead
volunteering for aviation crew duty as observers or gunners—service that
was equally hazardous. One Aggie to enlist in the naval ranks as a quartermaster was Thomas C. Holliday '15 from El Paso. He joined the Corps
of Cadets and spent a couple of years in college before returning home
to work in the local dry goods store, Krakauer, Zork & Moye's, to earn
enough money to return. He, like Easterwood, enlisted upon hearing of
the declaration of war. While on a low-level German U-boat hunting
patrol in a navy seaplane over the North Sea on May 6, 1918, Holliday
survived the most dangerous event of his entire assignment.[9]

Holliday, who was manning his observation position in the slow-
moving seaplane, was trying to mark the location of an enemy submarine. The pilot, Ensign Herbert Lasher of Tivoli, New York, later recalled,
"I had swerved the plane at an acute angle in a sudden turn. My engine
went dead. It was a heavy bombing machine and with the engine disabled
I couldn't get her back even. She started to fall. I managed to spiral a little
and then lost control. She crashed into the sea at a terrific speed. It was an
awful smashup. Believe me, it's as bad hitting water as land."[10]

His co-pilot, Ed A. Smith, "died outright and sank. He never came
up." Ensign Lesher was knocked unconscious with a broken leg. "I don't
remember anything for several minutes; when I came to, Holliday was
holding me onto a piece of the wreckage." Holliday had been thrown
clear of the site and, despite two broken legs and massive wounds, swam
back to the wreckage and dove into it in an effort to save the pilot, who
was about to sink a second time. He held the pilot's head above the water
line for over an hour until a second patrol seaplane flying in the same
area returned to find the two men floating in the wreckage. Without

radio communications, the returning plane released two carrier pigeons with a message to base to send for boats to "bring us in" (interestingly, pigeons were faster than planes). From "somewhere in France" Ensign Lasher, in recovery, noted, "I owe my life to Tom Holliday of Texas." For his heroic actions, Tom was awarded the Navy Cross.[11]

Quartermaster Thomas C. Holliday
Observer, French Aviation Unit, Naval Aviation
Date of Action: May 8, 1918
Citation: The president of the United States of America takes pleasure in presenting the Navy Cross to Quartermaster First Class Thomas C. Holliday, US Navy, for extraordinary heroism and devotion to duty while servicing in the French Unit, US Naval Forces. On May 6, 1918, the seaplane in which he, with two officers, had been making an antisubmarine patrol, was wrecked near Dunkirk. In spite of injuries to himself, Quartermaster First Class Holliday dived repeatedly to rescue the officers.

Unarmed and Unafraid

Almost all the hands-on training for observation-scout missions was conducted in France. During the early months of the air war, both the French and British gained a great deal of experience with air-to-air tactics, as well as knowledge of situations and enemy tactics to avoid. When instructed by the French on tactics, pilots of slow-moving observation planes were encouraged to do all they could to complete the mission. Their briefing was blunt: "Your plane will be slower, less maneuverable [2 crew, heavy wireless transponder, and bulky cameras]—if attacked do not hesitate to run!" Enemy aircraft sought out these observation planes, especially in advance of a German offensive, making them perfect prey for faster and more maneuverable fighters. And when retreat was impossible, one had to stand and fight.[12]

Many harrowing stories of bravery emerged from air combat over France. Capt. Charles T. Trickey '17 never had a routine mission as he flew multiple, unarmed reconnaissance missions behind enemy lines in a French-designed, bi-wing Darand AR.1 to monitor enemy troop movements and warn the Allies of pending German attacks. The maze of

Figure 22. The heroic actions of Captain Charles Trickey '17 saved his crippled and burning airplane and the pilot, earning him the Silver Star. 1917 *Longhorn* yearbook, courtesy of Cushing Memorial Library & Archives, Texas A&M University.

CHARLES T. TRICKEY
SANGER

Civil Engineering

Age, 21; Major First Battalion First Regiment; Chairman Senior Election Committee; Longhorn Staff; Manager Junior Battalion 1915-16.

CAPTAIN Muller's best soldier boy,

THE most chivalrous gallant of the

"CHILLIE-Million railroad gang,"

THE "Old General's" Municipal

ENGINEER, will soon take a job as

RECRUITING officer of the Hoss

MARINES, office Forsythe Building,

CHICAGO.

trenches and camouflage along the mile-wide front made it necessary to fly low and slowly to collect creditable intelligence and photographs. The low altitude also exposed the plane to intense ground fire. During one such treetop mission, an incendiary bullet passed through the fuselage, igniting the gas tank and spreading fuel and flames between the pilot in the front seat and Trickey in the back. As burning fuel poured into the compartment, Trickey climbed onto the wing, hoping to assist the pilot in landing the plane behind their own lines. As the pilot came to a full stop in friendly territory, Trickey entered the flaming wreckage to pull the pilot to safety. The pilot died within hours and Trickey, despite burns on his hands and lower arms, soon was back in the air, alone, headed for combat along the front lines. For his heroism, he received the Silver Star.[13]

Captain Charles T. Trickey
Observer, 88th Aero Squadron, AEF
Date of Action: September 28, 1918
Citation: By direction of the president, Captain (Air Service) Charles T. Trickey, United States Air Service, is cited by the Commanding General, American Expeditionary Forces, for gallantry in action and a Silver Star placed upon the ribbon of the Victory Medals awarded him. Captain Trickey distinguished himself by gallantry inaction while serving as an Observer with the 88th Aero Squadron, AEF, in action near Nantillois, France, September 28, 1918, while on an infantry contact mission.

A month after Captain Trickey's action over enemy lines, Lt. Mitchell H. Brown '16 from Rockwall, Texas, became engaged in an action similar to that experienced by Trickey. Ordered overseas in January 1918, Brown was sent to French artillery school prior to transferring to the aviation school at Chatillon-Sur-Seine as a flight instructor. Following orientation, he was assigned to the 50th Aero Squadron, 1st Corps Observation Group as an observer-gunner. Like Trickey, he quickly learned that nothing was routine. While on a reconnaissance mission near Beffu-et-le-Morthomme on October 23, 1918, his pilot, Lt. George R. Phillips, attacked and downed a German observation balloon. Within minutes, three German Fokker fighters counterattacked at very close range. Incendiary bullets from the enemy penetrated the plane's thin skin, igniting the signal rockets under Brown's seat. Disregarding the flames, Brown continued his fire, destroying one German plane and forcing the others to break off action. With quick action, the fire was extinguished and the mission to collect intelligence completed. Reflecting on the air action over France, Brown wrote his wife, Lilybel, "It's all very true war isn't what it's cracked up to be. Lots of times you have a longing for quiet pastures when the odds loom up against you. Personally, I had rather die a dozen times than to have folks say I didn't do my duty." For their calm and courageous actions, Brown and Phillips were awarded the Distinguished Service Cross.[14]

Lt. Mitchell H. Brown
Observer, 50th Aero Squadron, AFE
Date of Action: October 23, 1918
Citation: The president of the United States takes pleasure in presenting the Distinguished Service Cross to Lt. (Air Service) Mitchell H. Brown, for extraordinary heroism in action while serving with the 50th Aero Squadron, AEF, near Beffu-et-la-Morthomme, France, October 23, 1918. Lt. Brown, observer, piloted by Lt. Phillips, while on reconnaissance for the 78th Division, attacked as enemy balloon and forced it to descend. They were in turn attacked by three enemy planes. The incendiary bullets from the enemy's machine set the signal rockets in Lt. Brown's cockpit afire. Disregarding the flames, he continued to fire, destroying one enemy plane and forcing the others to retire. They successfully completed their mission and secured valuable information.

Day-to-day aero squadron combat activities intensified after September 1918. By this time, large numbers of trained pilots and new aircraft increased the capacity of Allied operations along the Western Front. The expansion of missions is seen in the sorties flown by Texas Aggie Lt. Martin C. Giesecke '12 of San Antonio. The eldest son of famed Texas A&M architect Frederick E. Giesecke, Class of 1886, he was schooled in music from an early age and played saxophone in the Texas Aggie Band. As a cadet, he was an expert marksman and a member of the Veterans of the Lost Cause and the Bow-Legged Club. After earning a degree in chemical engineering, Giesecke returned to San Antonio as a production manager at Liberty Mills. Shortly after the declaration of war, he resigned and joined the Enlisted Reserve Corps (ERC) in May. After SMA and basic flight training at Kelly Field, he was commissioned as a lieutenant in September 1917 and sent to advanced training with the RAF in London before assignment to the 17th Aero Pursuit Squadron in France. Cleared for combat flights, he began near-daily missions on September 3, 1918.[15]

Lieutenant Giesecke, nicknamed "Gesooks," was popular and quick to ease the pervasive tension with down-home, Texas anecdotes and amenities that improved camp life. The official history of the 17th Squadron noted that he "stepped into the breach" by rigging wire net and an unserviceable blowpipe into a toaster for the mess hall, after which he was called "O. C. Toast." His contributions, however, far exceeded his skill at contriving small appliances. He flew daily combat sorties deep into enemy territory. A sample of these missions, flown in a bi-wing Sopwith Camel by Giesecke and the 17th Squadron, provides a good window into the flight operations:[16]

Figure 23. Lt. Martin C. Giesecke '12 was first trained in England and assigned to the 17th Aero Pursuit Squadron flying over two dozen missions in a Sopwith Camel. Courtesy of Cushing Memorial Library & Archives, Texas A&M University.

Figure 24. Pilot training in England was in the tiny Sopwith Camel F-1. Often a handful to fly, over 5,500 were produced. The small craft was well suited for scout missions, with wood wings covered with fabric, a maximum speed of 115 mph, a rate of climb of 1,100 feet per minute, and a ceiling of 21,000 feet. Courtesy of Wilson Collection.

Other Texas A&M alumni who were observation pilots over France and Germany in 1918 included Lt. William T. Donoho '13, Lt. Roderick R. Allen '15, Lt. Joel I. McGregor '16, Lt. Roy L. Young '16 (wounded in action), and Lt. Eben H. Mills '13, with the 258th Observation Squadron. Ground crews and mechanics formed a lasting bond with the pilots they supported. These airman were expected to keep planes flying and took pride in their work, with one aviator noting to a visiting reporter: "He called attention with pride to the tiny Maltese or 'iron crosses' cloth patches glued on the wings and fuselage of the airplane—marking the spots where shrapnel and machine gun bullets had torn perilously near to the pilot and observer and where the repairs have been made by mechanics who were jealously proud of the little insignias of narrow escapes. One plane bore more than twenty such 'iron' cross-patches in one small part of the fuselage."[17]

N'est ce pas?

By early 1918, American training facilities produced more pilots, observers, and mechanics. Twins Edward and Roger Brown of the Class of 1917

Table 5. Lt. Giesecke western front flight ops: September–October 1918

Date	Target	Plane	Altitude	Action
Sept. 27	Bapaume	Sopwith, D	3,000 feet	2–20 lb. bombs
Sept. 27	Canal de l'Escaunt	Sopwith, B	2,500 feet	4–20 lb. bombs
Sept. 29	Cambrai	Sopwith, D	3,000 feet	Bombs and strafing
Sept. 29	Honnecourt	Sopwith, D	2,000 feet	4–20 lb. bombs
Oct. 1	Awoingt	Sopwith, F	3,000 feet	4–20 lb. bombs
Oct. 2	Awoingt	Sopwith, F	3,000 feet	4–20 lb. bombs
Oct. 2	Awoingt	Sopwith, D	3,000 feet	4–20 lb. bombs
Oct. 3	Caudry RR	Sopwith, D	5,000 feet	4–20 lb. bombs
Oct, 5	Awoingt	Sopwith, D	5,000 feet	4–20 lb. bombs
Oct. 7	Awoingt	Sopwith, D	5,000 feet	4–20 lb. bombs
Oct. 8	Cambrai	Sopwith, F	1,000 feet	Bomb and strafing
Oct, 8	Cambrai RR	Sopwith, D	900 feet	Strafing troops
Oct, 9	Awoingt and Cauroir	Sopwith, D	5,000 feet	4 bombs
Oct. 9	St. Hoaire	Sopwith, D	5,000 feet	1–20 lb. bombs

Note: The Sopwith Camel had a range of 300 miles, a ceiling of 21,000, and maximum speed of 115 miles per hour.

were commissioned with their class at Leon Springs, attended ground school at the Austin Aeronautical Center, and were sent to advanced flight training in England and, from there, onto Camp Ovesto, Foggia, Italy. The Browns were among some 300 American aviators and crew members stationed in Italy throughout the war. Roger Brown would become a ferry plane pilot along with Ensign Easterwood and Lt. Marion Daugherty '16. Additional Aggies at Foggia included Lt. Guy N. Adriance '15, Lt. Harvie R. Matthews '20, and mechanic Pvt. Bettis Moore, '20. Lt. Edward Brown was transferred back to France to serve as a pilot and observer with the 166th Bombardment Squadron. He was awarded the Silver Star for "efficient and hazardous" flight over enemy positions during the Meuse-Argonne offensive in October 1918. Other aviators engaged in the Meuse-Argonne engagement included Lt. John Adams Langston '12 of Cleburne with the 644th Aero Squadron, who remained on Air Service active duty during the postwar years to assist with the Hungary Direct Relief Program in 1919.[18]

When war was declared, Lt. Cyrus Earle Graham '16 of Bryan was assistant entomologist with the Texas State Department of Agriculture in Austin. As the war progressed and Graham considered military service, Agricultural Commissioner Fred W. Davis encouraged him to remain in his job. Regardless of his duties in Austin and not wanting to be considered a "slacker," Graham enlisted in the Air Service in July 1917. He completed ground school in Austin and was transferred to France for flight training.[19]

In a letter to his brother DeWitt, Earle recounted the ever-present dangers and his brush with death. Graham disclosed that a malfunction in his aircraft "was my own fault [stunt flying] and I learned a great deal in a few minutes." He had lost control and was spinning to a "bad landing consisting of a fall of 2,500 feet!" Detailing the final seconds of the flight, he noted, "Some fall I would say. There was no nervous shock but it was an awful shock when I ran into old Mother Earth. When the thing hit

Figure 25. This crashed Breguet Br 14 was one of the most effective French fighters. Deployed to the front in November 1917, it was one of the first with a metal air frame, maximum speed 110 mph, and ceiling of 18,000 feet. Courtesy of Wilson Collection.

I crawled out of what was left of the plane, took off my gloves, helmet, and put my fingers in my mouth, straightened my [broken] jaw and then walked to a French farm house about a half mile away."

Other planes overhead saw him crash and flew back to the airfield to dispatch an ambulance. Graham noted,

> I broke my shoulder, my lower jaw on both sides and cut my eyelids. My face was about the size of a bucket. [In the hospital] My teeth are laced together and then tied to the upper ones and for a few weeks I lived on eggnog, milk, and thin soup. The doctors worked on my shoulder, fixed my eye, and jaw . . . classy to have three specialists work on you—*n'est ce pas?*—Isn't that so? It is not every day you can fall 2,500 feet and be up walking a few minutes later—I am very thankful to be alive and really feel that I owe Him my life.

His parting words to his brother in the letter were: "I shall be glad to get back flying once more. I wish you could see some real fliers and with machines so small you think you could pick one up. You people must not worry. When your time comes you must go and not before." Lieutenant Graham was soon back in the cockpit. Just two days before the Armistice, on November 9, 1918, he was killed in a crash. He was returned to Texas in November 1920 for internment. The American Legion Post in Bryan is named in his honor.[20]

Attack Pilots

Clyde N. Bates '17 of El Campo volunteered directly in the US Marine Corps in June 1917, followed by officer training at Quantico, Virginia, and commissioning as a second lieutenant. He was recommended for pilot training at Lake Charles, Louisiana, followed by NAS Miami. He was sent to France for advanced training as a bomber pilot with the Joint Foreign Service Unit. Upon completing advanced instruction on checkouts and tactical training with the French, he flew dozens of missions with the First Marine Aviation Force. His primary mission prior to the Armistice was enemy interdiction using Curtiss N-9 and Curtiss R-6 floatplanes along the Dover Straits area of the English Channel and the Belgium front in the St. Pol and St. Oman sections opposite Ypres. Lieutenant Bates' distinguished service operating against an enemy logistic network was recognized with the Navy Cross in November 1918.[21]

Lt. Clyde Noble Bates
First Marine Aviation Force
Date of Action: September-November 1918
Citation: The president of the United States of America takes pleasure in presenting the Navy Cross to First Lieutenant Clyde N. Bates,
United States Marine Corps, for distinguished and heroic service as
an Aviator of an aeroplane while serving with the First Marine Aviation Force, attached to the Northern Bomb Group (USN), in active
operation cooperating with the Allies Armies on the Belgian Front
during September, October, and November, 1918, bombing enemy
bases, aerodromes, submarine bases, ammunition dumps, railroad
junctions, etc.

Bates completed his tour of duty in Marines Corps aviation in March
1919 as a captain and returned to El Campo, Texas, to work in his family business. In the early 1930s, he moved to Houston to be a manager
at Longhorn Cement Company (the same company that later employed
Joseph E. Routt '38, Texas A&M's first two-time, All-American football
star).[22]

While not a former student or degree-holding Texas Aggie, one "associ-
ate" member of the Texas A&M family listed in all the alumni directories
as an honorary member of a number of A&M graduating classes was the
venerable football coach Dana Xenophon Bible. Born and raised in Jeffer-
son City, Tennessee, he began one of the most heralded coaching careers
in the first half of twentieth century. After coaching briefly at Louisiana
State University, Bible came to A&M in 1916 to coach the freshman team.
His success was immediate and sustained. At the age of 25, he won the
first of three Southwest Conference Championships in the fall of 1917
with arguably the greatest team in the university's history. The cadets went
undefeated, untied, and unscored against, racking up 270 points against
their scoreless rivals. Following the 7–0 victory over archrival Texas Long-
horns in their annual Thanksgiving Day game, Bible enlisted in the US
Army (interestingly, he listed his profession on his Brazos County draft
registration card not as coach at the A&M College but as "instructor and
student advisor").[23]

Aviation Cadet Bible was prequalified to attend ground school at the School of Military Aeronautics in Austin and went on to earn his wings at Carruthers Field in Fort Worth. In mid-1918, he was sent to France with the 22nd Aero Squadron, known as the "Shooting Stars" of the 1st Field Army. In addition to flying pursuit missions, Bible passed the time in France coaching airmen in intersquad football and baseball games, a popular pastime. The Aggie coach recalled that his teams in France had some of the top All-American college players from the Ivy League, the South, and Texas. Bible returned to the A&M campus in the spring of 1919, along with many of the Aggie players who had enlisted in the army, and immediately began recruiting and training the team for the fall '19 season. The old "pep" and enthusiasm of the prewar campus soon returned, and the Aggie football team fielded championship squads in 1919 through 1921.[24]

Crusaders of the Air

The massing for General Pershing's largest frontal offensive on the Western Front in the fall of 1918 resulted in the greatest concentration of Air Service missions to date. The increase in sorties across the lines was met

Figure 26. Captured enemy aircraft were always a big prize: the caption reads "hunting Fokker after its capture." The model was the primary aircraft of the German Air Service, maximum speed 120 mph with an 180 hp Mercedes D.IIIa engine and a ceiling of 7,000 feet. Courtesy of Wilson Collection.

with a full force response from the German Luftwaffe. The terror in the skies and the loss of friends in aerial combat is described vividly by Lt. Hal Irby Greer '03 in his detailed and emotional letter to his mother in Beaumont, Texas:

Somewhere in France, September 14, 1918
Mother Dear:

Your little boy has had some wild times today and for three days past. I have been engaged in some of the hardest and most dangerous work that we have. I was to have done some patrol work with Rueben in our ship in conjunction with spod [Spud] fighters, but our ship was bad in the motor so we escaped that.

But this morning I had the sensation of all sensations. We penetrated far into Germany on a bombing trip, though my bombs weren't attached to the plane, for which I am duly thankful as you will learn later. I was put out on the rear guard of the formation and [Lt.] Rueben [D. Biggs] and I had our work cut out I assure you! In the first place we had to put up with the most severe "archie" [anti-aircraft] fire which is terrible. First you hear a "rack-crack," and a smoke ball opens up in your rear somewhere, then the next one is over you. Then under you, then to the side of you, all the time biting closer and closer! God! What a feeling! It's terrible! Then finally you hear one "c-r-r-a-S-H!" after another, and you know they're horribly close! You can't dodge, you just stand there and watch these ominous balls of smoke. I steadied myself by counting them and thinking. "Well if only one hits me from above, it will probably be in the head and I won't know it, so what's the use?" Then I asked God to forgive all my past, and if it be His will to make me at least die like a man and protect my two boys and brother. Then the "archie" fire let up, just as we reached our objective. We dropped our bombs, those of us who carried them and I knew something was coming! It did alright!

The "Richtofen [sic] Circus" jumped us. Lord, but the air was full of "boches" [slang for German soldiers] They dived on us over my right shoulder, you see, as I explained, we were flying in the rear and on the extreme left [of the formation.] They divided us up and a bunch took each plane. Three swung round the back of me. I stood up high so as to protect Rueben's head with my body and waited for them to come in. Two were to one side and beneath me and the other was on one side and beneath me. They had red noses and all sorts of fantastic colors. The three of them opened up and got me in a cross fire, and I could see the bullets (tracer and incendiary) flashing all round me. I singled one

L'escadrille des "TANGOS" du L. Richtoffen.

Figure 27. A copy of this captured photo was acquired by Pvt. J. V. Wilson at the end of the war. Pictured is Baron von Richtoffen's L' Escadrille squadron, the famous "Tango Circus." Note the unique markings for each pilot of each fuselage. Courtesy of Wilson Collection.

out, and put my guns on him. My first burst was in front and high, so I corrected my aim, this time shooting low and behind. Then I swung my guns up deliberately 'till I saw his ship. He shot up straight in the air and I saw his orange colored belly, then he fell over on his back and straightened out on his long, long, long dive for the ground, which was two miles away [10,000 feet]. I thought at first he was pulling some trick, but I soon saw I had him.

Meanwhile the other two were making it hot for me, and I kicked the rudder, and pointed them to Rueben. He swung the ship, and I swung my gun over and opened up on another one of them. As soon as I did they dived off and quit, and the "scrap" was over.

One of our ships was shot down, I think by "archie" fire, and I turned around to count up those who were missing. We came on home and found six shrapnel holes under the engine and twelve bullet holes in the plane. Most of them were within six to eight feet of us, so you see we had it pretty warm. But your little boy has the honor of getting the first "boche" for the 11th Aero Squadron! You'd have thought it a devil of a show the way the boys all hugged me when they found out. Two others in the formation saw me get him, so they gave me the credit all O.K. But I was lucky, and while they came up I asked God to help me shoot straight and avenge a bosom friend of mine who was killed yesterday [September 13, 1918] by the dirty hounds. We were "frat" brothers and entered ground school, almost yesterday, it seems to me, together. His name was Bob Thompson, from Temple, Tex. Now I've another to get for Dick Moody, a good pal and friend of mine.

The way it looks now I won't make many more trips, mother dear; just know if they should get me that your son hasn't gone back on his blood from either side of the house, and that I'll go trying my best. I will try to scribble you a note each day until this terrible business is over. But we've got to "carry on." All I hope is dear James [Greer's brother] won't get into it in time. I must go now and get my guns cleaned and oiled and limbered up for another trip. With all my love.[25]

Your son 'till the end,
Hal Irby

Hal I. Greer, 1st Lt. ASSC
11th Aero Squadron
APO, No 703, A.E.F., France

Lt. Hal Greer continued to fly until the Armistice, although constant exposure to high-altitude, freezing conditions damaged his lungs. His mother captured his experiences in the air over there in verse, in a note from home labeled, "For Hal from mother:"

> Triune of love, and life, and might,
> Direct Thy soldiers in their flight.
> Oh Father, Son and Holy Ghost
> Strengthen Thy brave ascending host,
> With love, faith, consolation, care
> For Thy bold Crusaders of the air![26]

National Leader

Texas A&M was recognized nationally for its transformation in support of the war and the vast contributions of its students, former students and staff, and the thousands of army trainees who passed through its gates. In addition to the extensive campus training programs, by mid-1918 the college received a great deal of attention and praise for the service to the nation made by Texas Aggies. Former students were involved with all aspects of the war, across all the armed services. Many staff members

were called to war-related jobs, such as Agricultural Extension Director
Clarence Ousley, who became assistant secretary in the US Agricultural
Department to oversee food supplies and shipments. The magnitude of
Texas A&M's service first became news in the fall of 1918: 1,963 A&M
men were on duty, including 648 graduates (alumni), and 1,315 former
students. The number of Aggies in uniform grew to over 2,300. For a
number of weeks, *The New York Times* carried stories on the war contributions of "college men" from across the nation, initially stating that
the overwhelming majority of these men were from Yale, West Point, and
Texas A&M. In July, the *Times* noted that A&M "led all American colleges
in the percentage of alumni in military service."[27]

These reports were followed with feature stories of heroic actions that
filled the papers statewide. In addition to the contributions of the 250
Aggie aviation troops in France and stateside, decorated veterans of the
Western Front in France included Maj. Bennet Puryear '06, US Marine
Corps, Navy Cross; Lt. Henry W. Whisenant '16, DSC; former A&M staff
favorite Col. Ike Ashburn, DSC; Lt. Drinkard B. Milner '17, Silver Star;
and posthumously, the DSC awarded to Lt. John H. Moore '15. In total,
eleven A&M former students received the Distinguished Service Cross
and five the Navy Cross. Numerous Aggies received Silver Stars, and hundreds were wounded in action.[28]

5

COMING HOME
Postwar Aggieland

Thus in this great crisis of history the College vindicated the wisdom of
the statesmen who conceived the Morrill Act in making military training
a requirement of the curriculum. The College furnished over 2,300 well
trained officers for the service, fifty-five [63] of whom died in action.[1]

—Clarence Ousley
December 1, 1935

By late October 1918, troops "over there" and headlines in papers across
Europe and America speculated that the war might end by Christmas. The
influenza epidemic waned in early November, and, at home, people across
the country focused on a massive war bond drive to support the war effort. Through the first week of November, tens of thousands of newly
drafted troops took the train to New Jersey and New York, awaiting pas-
sage to Europe. This massive call-up was part of a plan to swell the army
ranks for a major Allied offensive to push the Hun out of the stalemated
trenches on the Western Front and invade Germany by the spring of 1919.
By early November, Texas alone had more than 180,000 men in uniform,

Figure 28. The German Albatros D.V was the primary fighter in early 1918. The 160 hp Mercedes DIII inline piston engine had a maximum speed of 105 mph and a ceiling of 18,000 feet. This was the personal biplane of Prince Frederick Karl of Prussia, commander of an artillery spotting unit. He was shot down and captured March 21, 1917. Wounded by friendly fire, he died on April 6, 1917. Courtesy of Wilson Collection.

as well as numerous women volunteers in the medical corps and administrative services.

Following the Allies' success on the Western Front at points like St. Michel, the Aisne-Marne salient, and Chateau-Thierry, the general staffs were ordered to expand plans for the next offensive. One critical element of the late 1918 buildup in France and England was the rapid increase in the number of aeroplanes and crew training in preparation to dominate the sky over the front, as well as extend bombing operations into the German heartland to disrupt transportation systems and attack military supply depots and utilities. Aircraft production bottlenecks in America delayed the delivery of new planes. Meanwhile, by the mid-October 1918, extensive negotiations to bring the war to an end were begun, with President Woodrow Wilson sending his personal representative, Col. Edward House, to France to open peace negotiations leading to an armistice and unconditional surrender by Germany. Europe, after more than 4 million deaths, was weary of war. The willingness of the Axis powers to halt the war would be over a month in the making.[2]

Citizen Soldiers

Texas A&M's participation in the war both at home and abroad had been exemplary. During the war, the Association of Former Students alumni organization authorized a 15 × 26 foot banner of the "best quality bunting" for the college's memorial "service flag." Around its periphery were more than 2,300 stars representing each A&M man in service, and a special center square of gold stars represented those who made the supreme sacrifice. It first hung in Guion Hall and later was moved to the rotunda of the Academic Building, where it remained through World War II. In the late 1960s it was placed in storage, then recovered and displayed in the alumni center before being transferred to the Cushing Library Archives for restoration.

As in all wars, uncertainty reigned. A clear, concise plan and direction forward were at the mercy of unforeseeable situations resulting from, among other things, weather conditions, access to resources, and the political will of those sending their own citizens to fight—and, too, on the willingness and morale of these citizens' soldiers to fight and die, when most had no clear idea what the conflict was about in the first place.

This is not to imply that most in uniform were aware of, or coached on, the meaning of their duty and obligation to serve that brought them face to face with a war not of their choosing. One aspect that cannot be minimized was the thrill of being "in the fight" with their comrades. This led to the rise of an *esprit de corps* among the troops through allegiance to their units and friends and their efforts to survive and persevere. Aware that there was an announcement was pending on the end of hostilities, unofficial victory celebrations began before the official notification of war's end on November 11. For many, the bonds of friendship and camaraderie began long before the war, as is underscored in a letter in the A&M *Alumni Quarterly*: "The A. and M. Spirit Follows the Fellows to France," submitted by Lt. Dillon T. Stevens '13:

SOMEWHERE IN FRANCE—November 10, 1918—

If you could look in on us tonight and forget where we were, you might easily imagine its gathering of some of the old boys in the College Mess, except that our uniforms are olive drab instead of cadet blue [gray]. The cloth is as white, the silver as gleaming and the food as good as at some of the special spreads that Bernard Sbisa used to set for us. In fact, the atmosphere of old A. and M. pervades this high ceiling dining room in

France tonight, and its walls have echoed to a "Chigaroo garem" and to "Rough tough, real stuff" in good old A. and M. style. Possibly the waiters think we have gone crazy or that perhaps we have heard through some private channel that the Kaiser has committed suicide. At any rate they do not understand "*Zese droll Americaines*" but you would and you'd know how good we feel to be here together.

Most of us are at a big flying field not many kilometers from here, while a few others ate at nearby posts. Some others missed being here by a narrow margin; for instance [Lt. W. Lee] "Fanny" Coleman left just a few days ago and though we've not heard, we hope he has Hun or so to his credit by now. [Lt. George I. '14] Lane pulled out last week and took his tin lid with him, so he must have some important business to attend to. [Lt. Roderick R.] "Red" Allen is not many kilometers distant, but we were unable to reach him with a notice of this rather impromptu spread.

We have with us tonight three of our ancient enemies, Lt. Ben H. Rice, Jr., Lt. Fred C. Roberts, and Lt. Frank M. Martin of the University of Texas, and they have contributed both to the merriment of the evening and to the zest of the reminiscences, particularly ancient football scores and student battles.

Regards to Sergeant Kenny [A&M commandant's staff], and to the other sergeants with him, who we know are keeping up with 2,000 A. and M. men in the Service, and are turning out new ones all the time.

Figure 29. Lt. Quinlan Adams '12 from Bryan, Texas, was active in organizing former cadet reunions in France. Courtesy of Cushing Memorial Library & Archives, Texas A&M University.

Now we will pledge A. and M and you and all our brothers over-there and over-here in the wine of France.

"Hold 'em A. and M."
[signed]

Lt. C. H. Harrison '12	Lt. J. M. Kendrick '15
Lt. Mark P. Thomas '17	Lt. W. T. Donoho '13
Capt. C. A. Biggers '14	Lt. Dillon T. Stevens '13
Capt. R. B. Pearce '11	Lt. Martin M. Daugherty '16
Lt. T. K. Morris '16	Lt. John Fries '12
Lt. Quinlan Adams '12[3]	

Homecoming

The guns fell silent at 11 PM on the eleventh day of the eleventh month, launching the legacy of World War I that forever changed the physical landscape and vision of the A&M College of Texas. More importantly, an entire generation of Aggies had a new perspective following the war. The A&M College Aggies, as well as millions of veterans from across America, gained a new view of the world that previously had been limited to their hometown or state. Many A&M cadets prior to the war recalled that the farthest they had ever traveled was when they left home to go college. World War I not only introduced these Americans to the larger world, it also, in the case of this study, brought into the world one of the most profound innovations of the early twentieth century—sustained, manned flight—through the pioneering pilots, observers, gunners, and crew. By 1918, less than 15 years after the Wright brothers made their flight on a windy beach in North Carolina, aviation had captivated the public's imagination.

The war disrupted the education of thousands of Aggie students. President Bizzell released an open letter, "The Call to College," to heartily welcome veterans who had not completed their studies due to the conflict back to the A&M College:

The CALL to COLLEGE

The ending of the world war creates the obligation upon every young man to renew his college education. It was right for the young manhood of the nation to respond to the call to army service in behalf of the cause of human freedom and brotherhood. The issues were clearly conceived and the challenge was nobly accepted. The heroism of the American soldier has added another chapter to the glorious history of our country. But the war is over. The victory of arms is complete. New problems and new issues confront us. It would be a peril if we should fail to conceive of the great problems that confront the world in a task of reconstruction.

The call to college is addressed to you in this spirit. It is a personal invitation to each student whose work was interrupted by the call to arms to return and to resume his college course. Our college community awaits expectantly the return of those whom we have known as college students in the past years. We have thought and spoken of you often; we have followed your careers through army camps, on shipboard and overseas; we have waited with deep concern for the outcome of every battle because of the part some of you have played in this great game of human conflict. We have treasured every letter that you have written and every bit of news that has come to us concerning you and your former fellow students. A hearty welcome will await each of you on your return to college.

The course of study herewith submitted has been modified to meet as effectively as possible the needs of each student whose work has been interrupted by the war. The faculty has done everything possible to make the necessary adjustments to prevent any unnecessary loss of time because of conditions which have interrupted your normal college course. Unusual advantages will come to you through the adjustments that have been made. It is my earnest hope that every young man who ought to resume his studies here will not fail to take advantage of the opportunities that this course of study provides.

Sincerely yours,
W. B. Bizzell, President

The war's impact on the college soon became apparent. Almost immediately, the knowledge and experience gained from wartime flight operations and technological advancements, as well as other groundbreaking inventions from the war, altered the college's academic curriculum, research horizons, and industrial production processes and investments, and thus shaped the debate on how best to employ this new era of flight and allied pursuits. From flight came an entirely new thrust to improve and advance such items as engines, fuels, radio communications, new

aircraft designs, new materials, navigation enhancements, and metrolog-
ical forecasting, to determine the best of class and adoption for both private and commercial usage.

Texas A&M and other institutions across the country that had been
engaged in training, research, and assistance greatly benefitted from wartime advances. In the rapid draw down after the end of hostilities, the War
Department turned over most of its "training" equipment, apparatus, and
manuals to the institutions. In the case of A&M, this contributed in large
part to the rewriting of the curriculum in electrical engineering, mechanical engineering, and meteorology, and the introduction of a rash of new
courses known as "aeronautic studies." From these advances would come
new production procedures, chemical fertilizers, and machinery that advanced teaching and research in the field of agriculture as well.

Figure 30. Lt. Harry
B. Moses '18 was
stationed at Coblenz
Airdrome with the
138th Aero Squadron.
Note the very heavy
flight suit to combat
freezing temperatures
above 8,000 feet. Moses
Papers, courtesy of
Dolph Briscoe Center
for American History,
University of Texas at
Austin.

Figure 31. The French Harriot HD-3 was the result of new aerodynamic improvements. A two-seat fighter had a maximum speed of 120 mph. Not available until October 1918, it had enlarged ailerons and rudder which made the aircraft more maneuverable. Courtesy of Wilson Collection.

In June 1919, the War Department made the final federal reimbursement to the college for facilities and staff service, totaling $550,310.70. In sending its thanks the department noted, "We feel that not a single institution in the country has done a greater proportionate amount of effective war work." Both President Bizzell and engineering dean Bolton were congratulated for service rendered. One bonus was that the college was able to obtain additional surplus equipment the army no longer needed, which proved tremendous assistance for the college to continue special courses, extension work, and research.[4]

The Supreme Sacrifice

Blow again, bugle, blow once more—not the beautiful but sorrowing strains of Taps with which we laid him to rest—but the glorious notes of a divine Reveille for one who wakes to see the sun—for one who faces morning!

Robert Gordon Anderson
Not Taps, But Reveille, 1918

Figure 32. Coming home. Douglas W. Howell '19 of Bryan was inducted in the army and commissioned as a second lieutenant in the fall of 1918 shortly after being selected Cadet Corps Commander. He was on active duty preparing to deploy to France when the war abruptly ended on November 18, 1918. He was discharged in December and arrived back on campus to put on his senior boots and start class on January 3. Howell, pictured in his Cadet Colonel uniform, sits with his dog, Chummy. Courtesy of Ellen Howell Myers.

Table 6. Agricultural and Mechanical College of Texas Gold Book, 1917–1919

Deaths among A&M Aviation Service Members		
Name	Date	Notes
Major John W. "Billie" Butts '10	Apr. 3, 1919	Crash South Georgia
Lt. Jesse Easterwood '11	May 19, 1919	Crash in Panama
Lt. Cyrus E. Graham '16	Nov. 9, 1919	Plane crash in France
Lt. James F. Greer 'x14	Oct. 21, 1918	Crash at Issoudun
Lt. W. S. Keeling '20	Sept. 10, 1918	Crash at Carruthers Field
Lt. Willford McFadden 'x18	Oct. 7, 1918	KIA/MIA on patrol
Lt. John L. Matthews 'x08	Oct. 16, 1918	Auto crash in France
Lt. Harry L. Peyton 'x16	Mar. 18, 1918	Crash Kelly Field
Lt. Charles E. Rust 'x15	Oct. 10, 1918	KIA at the Front
Lt. William G. Thomas '19	Sept. 22, 1918	Crash Nancy, France
Capt. C. V. Woodman '06	Dec. 5, 1918	Pneumonia in California

Source: "Our Roll of Honor," *Alumni Quarterly*, November 1918, pp. 20–22; Gold Book, *Alumni Quarterly*, August 1919.
Note: The total loss of Texas A&M former students from 1917–1919 is estimated to be 63 and is listed with 54 names on the West Gate World War I Memorial, first located next to Guion Hall (today the site of Rudder Tower), moved c. 1970 to the West Gate entrance, and in 2015 relocated to the entrance of the Duncan Quad Corps area.

The rise of new pursuits and advancements in education and research were further augmented by the experience and drive of returning veterans who had the hands-on knowledge of the technology they encountered prior to returning to the classroom. Vocational training assistance for veterans was provided by the Smith-Sears Act of June 17, 1918, which allowed the college to expand courses and programs in industrial development and engineering extension. Texas A&M alone enrolled in a special postwar program for an initial group of 320 disabled veterans, which grew in numbers each month, as well as programs for new faculty and the hundreds of returning former students seeking to complete their degrees.[5]

The college transitioned to this new and expanded curriculum and postwar growth over some six months after the November 11, 1918, Armistice. Returning veterans and new cadets pushed the enrollment past 1,800 by June 1919, the largest in the college's history. And returning head football coach Dana X. Bible posted the first 10–0 season in the college's history, scoring 275 and holding all opponents scoreless, capped with a 7–0 victory over archrival University of Texas.

In addition to the Service Memorial Banner that hung in the Academic Building, the campus enacted a number of memorial traditions honoring those who served in the Great War. In the years following the conflict, the initial indication was that 54 Texas A&M former students were lost in service, yet it was later determined that 60 were lost. Prior to the correction of the record, 54 oak trees were planted around Simpson Drill Field, and American flags still fly on the perimeter of Kyle Field during home football games, representing those lost. Plans to build a memorial stadium on the site of Dean Kyle's farm patch were delayed for more than three decades due to a shortage of funding in the early 1920s, and the Memorial Student Center, the "living room of campus," was dedicated in 1951. In 1924, a nine-ton, granite-flag-draped memorial was dedicated by Governor Pat Neff in memory of Texas A&M's World War I sacrifice. First located on the site of Guion Hall (today Rudder Tower), the monument was moved to the West Gate entrance of the campus, then to the northwest corner of the drill field, and in 2015 was relocated to the entrance of the Quadrangle in the cadet housing area.[6]

Epilogue: The Next War

Many of the German people and leadership felt they had been betrayed and sold out by their government at a time when they could have won the Great War. This guilt or angst caused by their belief that they had been betrayed largely was the result of German politicians' "tactical blunder" in not working to prevent America's entry into the war, either by a quick victory prior to 1918, a truce, or any means to allow a victory. These events profoundly influenced German thinking and politics during the 1920s, contributing to the rise of Hitler in the 1930s, who set out to right the perceived injustice of Germany's November 1918 defeat and surrender. In mid-1919, a short article in the *Houston Post* unwittingly provided a harbinger of the future involving an incident reported by Lt. Frank W. Judd '18 of the 156th Field Artillery, 90th Division upon his return to Texas in June 1919.

Pinned to a shirt in the lieutenant's streamer trunk was a handwritten note in broken (but plain) English:

> Germany is not dead, she will rise up and strike, and she will rise again stronger than ever. She will be a mighty factor in the next war. I sincerely believe that a majority of people of Germany look forward to world domination as the outcome of the "next war." [7]

APPENDIX
Roster
Aggies in the Air Service

The following roster of Texas A&M former students who served in the Army, Navy, and Marine Air Service during World War I is the most complete to date, yet there are names that have escaped our research. Rank, name, class year affiliation at Texas A&M, and duty assignment are presented. The roster is divided into the following categories:

Army Air Service Deployed to Duty in the AEF—Europe
US Navy and Marines in the Air Service
Air Service Instructor Pilots and Crews in the United States
Air Service Maintenance, Crews, and Logistics
Commissioned Aviation Officers in Training
Noncommissioned Aviation Cadets in Training

Abbreviations:

Adv.: Advanced
AEF: American Expeditionary Force
ASSERC: Aviation Section Signal Enlisted Reserve Corps
Av.: Aviation
Av. Sect.: Aviation Section
BEF: British Expeditionary Force
Det: Detachment
ERC: Enlisted Reserve Corps
HQ: Headquartered
Inst.: Instructor
KIA: Killed-in-action
MIT: Massachusetts Institute of Technology
NAS: Naval Air Station
Obser.: Observation
RFC: Royal Flying Corps (UK)

Rplc: Replacement
SMA: School of Military Aeronautics
Sqdn.: Squadron
Ser.: Service
Trg.: training
USMC: United States Marine Corps

Army Air Service Deployed to Duty in the AEF—Europe

Lt. Quinlan Adams '12	France AEF July 1918–Jan. 1919
Lt. Henry A. Armstrong '18	British RFC / AEF (see pix)
Lt. Guy W. Adriance '15	Kelly Field / Camp Ovesto, Foggia, Italy
Lt. Roderick R. Allen '15*	1st Obser. Sqdn. Pilot
Lt. Dana X. Bible coach	SMA / Carruthers Field / 22nd Aero. Sqdn., France
Cpl. Pearce K. Barry '20	673rd Aero. Sqdn.
Lt. Robert D. Biggs 'x12	ASSRC
Lt. William H. Boothe '19	Wings / Kelly Field, Adv. Trg., France, Nov. 18
Lt. Mitchell H. "Reveille" Brown '16	Air Obser. DSC 50th Aero. Sqdn.
Lt. Edward L. Brown '17	Silver Star LS / Austin / NY to England to Camp Ovesto, Italy
Lt. Roger P. Brown '17	Leon Springs / SMA / to Camp Ovesto Foggie, Italy
Lt. Julius A. Cobolini 'x07	AEF: June 1918–January 1919
Lt. W. Lee Coleman 'x17	ASSRC
Lt. Marshall C. Crisp '16	SMA / Kelly Field, October 1918– February 1919
Lt. C. E. Crumrine '13	DFC: Postwar mission
1st Sgt. William C. Dodd 'x18	490th Aero. Sqdn.
Maj. Howard C. Davidson 'x11**	7th Av. Sqdn. / HQ Paris
Lt. William T. Donoho '13	Obser. specialist
Lt. Rufus R. Eddins '09	Av. Sect.

*World War II and Korea veteran, retired major general, US
**World War II veteran, retired major general, USAF

Lt. Martin M. Daugherty '16	April 17 Av. Sect. wounded AEF
Lt. Welboune O. Farthing '17	ASSRC
Lt. James W. Francis 'x18	Cmdt 17th and 152rd Aero. Sqdn. / CO Oxfordshire Airdome, England
Sgt. Louis Fries '13	139th Aero. Sqdn.
Lt. Martin C. Giesecke '12	17th Aero. Sqdn. (see pix)
Pvt. Thomas G. Gilley '23	297th Aero. Sqdn. / 1106 Aero. Rplc Sqdn.
Lt. Cyrus Earle Graham '16	Killed in crash Nov. 9, 1918
Pvt. Marshall P. Graves '19	376th Aero. Sqdn., Field no. 2, Hempstead, NY
Lt. James F. Greer 'x14	Killed Oct. 21, 1918 / France
Lt. Hal Irby Greer 'x03	10th Aero. Sqdn.
Lt. C. Harrell Harrison '12	AEF June 1918–July 1919
Lt. Ernest N. Henley '17	168th and 151st Aero. Sqdn.
Lt. Graily H. Higginbotham 'x16	ASSRC
Lt. Gordon F. Hinds 'x17	375 Aero. Sqdn.
Lt. Roy Eldon Keeling 'x16	50th and 636th Aero. Sqdn.
Lt. George I. Lane '14	Camp Funston, Kansas
Lt. John A. Langston '12	Meuse-Argonne Offensive
Pvt. James H. Leatherwood 'x16	ERC, 169th Aero. Sqdn.
Lt. Walter W. Lechner 'x14	169th Aero. Sqdn.
Lt. A. B. Lemond '19	637th and 116th Aero. Sqdn. AEF
Lt. Herbert M. Mason 'x18?	Pershing, Mexico 1915; 1st Def. of London RAF
Lt. Hervie R. Matthews '20	Av. Sect. Camp Ovesto, Foggia, Italy
Sgt. James G. Matthews 'x17	HQ 91st Aero. Sqdn.
Lt. John Lamar Matthews '08	17th Aero. Sqdn., killed trg. in France
Lt. Willford McFadden 'x18	KIA Oct. 7, 1918 / 103rd Aero. Sqdn. (Lafayette Escadrille)
Lt. Joel I. McGregor '16	5 mo. at Tours, France, Observer / 79th Aero. Sqdn.
Pvt. Alden D. Miller 'x18	169th Aero. Sqdn.

Lt. Eben Herbert Mills '13	RAF Trg. / 183th Sqdn. / 258th Aero. Obser. Sqdn.
Mech. Lawrence Q. Millender '20	194th and 120th Aero. Sqdn. / London and France
Pvt. Bettis Moore '20	Medical Det. 8th Aero. Sqdn., Ovesto, Foggia, Italy
Lt. T. Kyle Morris '16	24th Aero. Sqdn.
Lt. Harry B. Moses 'x18	SMA, Austin, 638th and 138th Aero. Sqdn.
Lt. Julius H. Nussbaum '13	Air. Ser. England, Gerstener, LA
Capt. Clarence Oliver '13	10th Aero. Sqdn. Dec. 17–May 19, 33rd Aero. Sqdn.
Lt. David H. Orand '13	ERC, AEF
Cpl. Clifford W. Ownby '19	169th Aero. Sqdn.
Pvt. John G. Paxton '?	640th Aero. Sqdn.
Lt. Stanley E. Perrin '17	ASSRC, AEF
Lt. Marney D. Perry 'x13	SMA Austin, AEF
Pvt. James E. Neeld, '?	89th Aero. Sqdn.
Sgt. Howell Nolte 'x18	26th Aero. Sqdn.
Lt. Charles E. Rust 'x15	Wounded KIA Oct. 10, 1918, 104th Aero. Sqdn.
Lt. J. Emerson Sain '19	ASSRC, AEF
Lt. Thomas R. Scott '19	ASSRC AEF Feb. 1918–Feb. 1919
Pvt. C. Neill Singleton '19	102rd Aero. Sqdn. AEF, Lafayette Escadrille
Lt. Cyrus F. Smythe '13	Pilot AEF / AQ N 18 p. 17
Sgt. Carl T. Sprague '19	490th Aero. Sqdn. (see photo)
Lt. Charles L. Snearly '10	167th Aero. Sqdn.
Lt. Dillon T. Stevens '13	AEF
Lt. John G. Swope '17	838th Aero. Sqdn. / Sinn Fein, Ireland
Lt. Lee T. Taylor '12	Engineering Reserve Corps AEF
Lt. Theodore W. Temple 'x17	SMA / Air Ser.
Lt. Mark P. Thomas '17	AEF
Lt. William G. Thomas '19	Killed in crash, Nancy, France, Jan. 7, 1919

Lt. Eugene C. Tips '13	A. S. Mil. Aero., AEF
Capt. Charles T. Trickey '17	Silver Star, wounded 88th Aero. Sqdn.
Lt. Roy E. Young '15	Aerial Observer, wounded
Pvt. Edgar F. Wilton 'x18	285th, 1102nd, 702nd Aero. Sqdn.
Capt. Walter M. Wotipka 'x17	US Av. Sect. Sig. Res. Corps

Aggies Aviators with the Canadian Royal Flying Corps

Lt. Samuel Hill 'x16	Canadian Royal Flying Corps London, England
Flt. Lt. LuVerne M. Mathewson 'x17	84th Canadian Trg. Sqdn. RFC London

US Navy and Marines in the Air Service

Mach. Mate Av. Ulmont S. Allison '24	NAS Hampton Roads, VA
C. Mach. Mate Av. Charles L. Beatty 'AM	NAS Pensacola, died Oct. 7, 1918
Lt. Jesse L. Easterwood '11	Navy Cross, RAF No. 214 (Handley Page)
CMQ Ernest J. Biskamp 'x19	NAD, Seattle, WA ('17 LH)
Lt. Clyde Noble Bates '17	Navy Cross, USMC No. 217 Sqdn. (DH4)
Ens. L. Bernard Bone '18	Trg. Graduate School, MIT
Mech. Mate Raleigh DeLong '15	Machinist, NAS, Pensacola
C. Mech. Mate AV Otis L. Downs	NAS, Pensacola
Ens. Leon M. Gilmore 'x19	Miami, Field / center '17 A&M football team
Ens. Gratz Bryan Gouger '21	Navy Air Station Los Angeles
Mech. 1st Clav. Lane C. Graham '19	MIT: NAS Pensacola
QM Bruce Harpole '20	AEF
QM 1st C. Thomas C. Holliday 'x15	Navy Cross, AEF
CQM Av. John H. Hutchings	8th Naval District New Orleans
CQM Av. Walter H. Lawrence '18	Navy Av. Det. Seattle, WA
Ens. Maher Moore '13	NAS Dunkirk, France
CQM Av. Milburn E. Nutt '?	MIT / NAS Miami, FL
Lt. Edmund L. Riesner '16	USMC KIA AEF

Lt. J. Thomas Rollins '21

US Navy, cadet trg. MIT, Boston, MA

Capt. Thomas R. Shearer '12

USMC, Marine Air Ser., Pensacola, FL

Ens. William J. B. Sullivan '22

Av. Trg. School, Norfolk, VA, NAS

Naval Cadets in Training

Cadet Harvey M. Amsler 'x18

Av. Trg. Pensacola, FL

Cadet L. Bernard Bone '18

Av. Graduate School, MIT, Boston

Cadet Jeff P. Royder '19

Av. Graduate School, MIT, Boston

Air Service Instructor Pilots and Crews in the United States

Lt. Col. Richard B. Barnitz '12

Chief Flight Inst., Love Field / CO, Post Field, OK

Cpl. Ambrose M. Beaver 'x14

244th and 632nd Aero. Sqdn. Kelly Field

Lt. George H. Beverly '19

SMA / Kelly Field / Inst. Souther Field, GA

Lt. Walter A. Black '09

461st and 111st Aero. Sqdn. Brooks Field, TX

Lt. Galitzan N. Bogel 'x08

20th Aero. Sqdn. Kelly Field

Lt. Norfleet G. Bone 'x21

ASSRC

Maj. John W. "Billie" Butts '10

Killed in crash April 3, 1919, south GA

Lt. Robert T. Cronau 'x21

Inst. Taliaferro Field, Texas (see pix)

Pvt. Gordon B. Davis '20

870th Aero. Sqdn. Kelly Field

QM Granville E. Davis '20

Goodyear Flying Field, Ohio

Lt. Ben Fordtran 'x13

Inst.: School Military Aeronautics Austin

Lt. Bertram E. Giesecke '11

Inst.: School Military Aeronautics / Kelly

Lt. John A. Graves '24

ASSRC

Lt. Roland L. Grissom '17

Inst. machine gunnery, Austin Graduate School

Pvt. Gabriel C. Harman '20	SMA Austin
Lt. Walter S. Keeling '20	Killed at Carruthers Field, plane crash
Lt. Hugh B. Killough '16	Air. Ser., Inst., Post Field, OK and Camp Dick
Lt. Harry C. Knickerbocker '18	Air. Ser. Inst. Adv. flying Payne Field, West Pt., MS
Lt. John H. Lorenz '13	ASSRC
Lt. Charles B. Martin '16	280th Aero. Sqdn. Rich Field, Texas
Lt. Raymond R. Massey 'x15	ASSRC Camp Dick, Texas
Lt. Joel I. McGregor '16	Sch. of Aerial Obser. Ft. Still, OK
Capt. Penrose B. Metcalfe '16	Flight Inst., Wilber Wright Field, Ohio
Lt. James V. Meyer '16	SMA, Inst. Gunnery, Austin
Pvt. Georeg C. Moffett '16 *	Kelly Field
Lt. Col. Douglas B. Netherwood '08 **	CMDT Dallas Av. Camp, Love Field [B.Gen. WWII]
Lt. Cliff B. Norwood '20	ASSRC
Lt. Harley M. Peace 'x11	Rich Field, TX
Pvt. David E. Rainey '19	633rd Aero. Sqdn. Kelly Field
Lt. Albert W. Robinson '19	Inst. Adv. flying/ Rockwall Field, San Diego, CA
Lt. Millard E. Rollins '14	ASSRC Inst., cross-county flight, Call Field, TX
Maj. Clinton W. Russell 'x12***	7th Aero. Sqdn.; Barron Field, Texas; CO Rich Field
Lt. Joe H. Smilie '18	SMA Austin Carruthers Field
Lt. Charles H. Thalmann '11	Chief Flight Inst. / Kelly and Penn Field, Austin

*Member Texas State Legislature: 1930 to 1962
**World War II veteran: retired as brigadier general, USAF
***World War II veteran, retired brigadier general, US

Air Service Maintenance, Crews, and Logistics

Pvt. Grady S. Appling 'x19	SMA University of Calif.
Pvt. Alvin Alexander '20	SMA Austin / Av. Det. Park Field, Tennessee
Cpl. Homer H. Avent '19	160th Aero. Sqdn. Park Field, Tennessee
Cpl. Henry L. Ballew 'x16	873rd Aero. Sqdn. Love Field
Pvt. Horace H. Benson, 'x10	328th Aero. Sqdn. Kelly Field
Lt. Val T. Billups 'x17	Flight Comm. 344th Handley Page
Pvt. James D. Browne '22	SMA/ 631st Aero. Sqdn.
Pvt. Price Cambell '13	814th Aero. Sqdn. and 28th Ser Corps
Pvt. Ben F. Chamberlain 'x11	286th and 272nd Aero. Sqdn.
Lt. Joe L. Culbertson '13	Av. Sec., Gen. Supply Depot, Middleton, PA
Lt. Warren G. Church '12	Austin / Gershner Field, Louisiana
Pvt. James H. Collins '13	SMA, MIT, Ft. Sam Houston, TX
1st Sgt. William F. Crothers 'x15	197th Aero. Sqdn. Love Field
Pvt. George A Davidson '20	SMA, aircraft mechanic, Austin, TX
Lt. Stanley F. Dolch '14	ERC, SMA Austin, Arcadia, CA
1st Sgt. Carl T. David 'x14	197th Aero. Sqdn. Love Field
Lt. Sam G. Epstein '07	SMA Ellington Field
Pvt. Joe G. Eiband 'x12	191st Aero. Sqdn. Ellington Field
Lt. James Mills Forsyth '12	MIT / Love Repair Depot / CO Machine Shop
Lt. Raymond S. Fouraker '14	Air Ser. / Radio school / Columbia University / Post Field
Lt. Maury B. Gilson 'x11	Love Field, Texas
Pvt. Jack C. Gilespie 'x17	West Point, MS
Pvt. Thadeus A. Greathouse 'x18	SMA / Av. Conc. Camp, Dallas
Cpl. Zebulan T. Hamilton 'x18	397th Aero. Sqdn. Camp Benbrook, Texas
Lt. Allen B. Hannay 'x12	239th Aero. Sqdn. Kelly and Dix Fields, Texas
Lt. Eugene L. Harrison '20	ASSRC
Lt. Samuel F. Hurt '18	ASA / Penna Field, Texas

Pvt. Lewis A. Jones 'x13	275th Aero. Sqdn. Taliaferro Field, Texas
Sgt. John L. Matthews 'x08	Kelly / Barron Field, Ft. Worth / 124th Aero. Sqdn.
Mech. Clyde A. Mills 'x17	197th Aero. Sqdn. Love Field
Lt. Charles P. Mueller 'x16	ASA Kelly Field
Sgt. Willard B. Muse '13	865th Aero. Sqdn. Love Field
SMaj. Clayton W. Powell '19	Av. Sec. 688th Aero. Sup. Sqdn., Kelly Field
Pvt. Emerald E. Schow 'x11	675th Aero. Sqdn. / SMA Berkeley
Pvt. Howard C. Sherman '?	877th Aero. Sqdn.
Pvt. Arthur L. Smith '18	Balloon Div. Ft. Omaha, NE
Lt. Homer Turner 'x18	141st and 241st Aero. Sqdn., Kelly Field
Mech. Carroll E. Ward 'x13	286th Aero. Sqdn., Ellington Field
Pvt. Henry B. Weir 'x19	ERC, Kelly Field.
Pvt. Robert B. Whitton 'x20	SMA Austin
Lt. William M. Wheless 'x14	ERC, Aero. Gen. Sup. Dep., Kelly Field
Capt. Edgar F. Wilton 'x18	Radio Det. / Ellington Field
Lt. C. L. Williford '11	Bureau of Military Aeronautics, Washington, DC

Commissioned Aviation Officers in Training

Lt. Overton Abernathy '20	Cadet, SCA, Austin
Lt. Elmer C. Allison 'x18	Av. training, killed in crash Feb. 22, 1919, California
Lt. Hardy M. Benson '18	SMA Love Field, Dallas, 6th Aero. Sqdn.
Lt. Eric W. Bingham '19	SMA Austin / HQ Det. Selfridge Field, Michigan
Lt. Jacob Born '18	Austin graduate school / pilot trg. Call Field, Wichita, TX
Lt. Carl F. Braunig '17	SMA Austin and Carruthers Field
Lt. Frank W. Cawthon '15	Av. Sec. Camp Dick, Texas
Lt. Warren G. Church '12	School of Aviation, Austin/ Gerstner Field, Louisiana

Pvt. Ransom J. Cole '16	SMA Austin, TX
Lt. James E. Gardner '22	Cadet, Call Field, Texas
Lt. William E. Farthing '14	Observer, Selfridge Field, Michigan
Lt. Wilber C. Foster '17	193rd Aero. Sqdn.
Lt. Carl P. T. Griesenbeck '18	Austin graduate school / Ellington Field / pilot inst
Lt. Robert A. Hall '16	Cadet, Camp Pike, AK
Lt. Mark A. Hamilton '20	Cadet Av., Kelly Field, SA
Cadet J. Rutledge Hill '13	Austin graduate school, Barron Field, Texas
Lt. Orvis D. Hunter '19	ASSRC 627th Aero. Sqdn., Kelly Field
Lt. Agee G. Kimbell '18	Cadet, School of Military Aeronautics, Austin
Lt. John E. Jones 'x18	ASSRC Rich Field, Texas
Lt. George D. Livingston '21	Av. Ser. Res. Corps
Pvt. William P. Mansker 'x17	SMA / 811th Aero. Sqdn.
Lt. James H. Maupin 'x13	ASSRC Kelly Field, No. 2
Pvt. Van Dyne McCaleb '20	850th Aero. Sqdn. Ellington Field, Texas
Lt. Penrose B. Metcalfe '16	ASSRC W. Wright Field, Ohio
Lt. James V. Meyer '16	Inst. SMA Austin
Lt. Allin Fowler Mitchell '09	SMA Austin, Post Field, Oklahoma
Lt. Lee D. Parks '11	Kelly Field / Aberdeen, WA, Log Camp No. 1
Lt. Harry L. Peyton 'x16	Killed in Kelly Field crash April 28, 1918
Maj. John H. Pirie '06	Kelly / CO at Aberdeen Proving
Lt. Lee C. Rountree '19	ASSRC Camp Dick, Texas
Pvt. Gustav A. Saper '15	252nd Aero. Sqdn. Ellington Field
Lt. William C. Sinclair '16	ASSRC Taliaferro Field, Texas
Lt. Harry H. Singletary '16	Cadet Ellington Field, Houston, 5th Aero. Sqdn.
Capt. Horace Soule 'x13	81st Aero. Sqdn., Kelly Field
Lt. Otto Staerker '18	ERC, Carlston, Field, Florida
Lt. Albion B. Taylor '13	ASSRC Camp Dick

Lt. Shelly G. Tarkington '18	Kelly Field, No. 2
Lt. Howard F. Tilson 'x17	ASSRC, SMA, Flight Inst. Bolling Field
Lt. Homer H. Turner 'x18	SMA Austin
Lt. Herbert J. von Rosenberg '12	ASSRC Chief Engineer Officer, Ellington Field
Lt. James Knox Walker '18	ASSRC Camp Dick / pilot
Lt. Carl L. Williford '11	ASSC, Div. Mil. Aero. Sup. Ser., Ellington Field
Sgt. Albin F. Wood '20	194th Aero. Sqdn. Ellington Field
Lt. Cony Unas Woodman '06	Died pneumonia, Riverside, CA, Dec. 1, 1918
Lt. Brooks R. Woolford 'x13	332nd and 272nd Aero. Sqdn. Ellington Field
Lt. Ralph Hudson Wooten '16*	SMA Austin, Kelly Field, Flight Inst. Love Field
Pvt. Carl A. Wiedekind 'x10	69th Aero. Sqdn.

*World War II veteran, retired as major general, USAF

Noncommissioned Aviation Cadets in Training

Cadet Leslie J. Arnold '19	SMA Austin
Cadet John M. Alderson '20	Av. Sec. Ellington Field, Houston
Cadet Fred G. Benkendorfor '21	Av. Sec. Ellington Field
Cadet W. H. James Collins '13	SMA Boston
Cadet Willian C. Craig 'x15	SMA Austin
Cadet Thomas J. Davis '18	SMA Barron Field, Texas
Pvt. James S. Denison 'x14	SMA Princeton, NJ, Ft. Sill, OK
Cadet Stanley F. Dolch 'x14	Balloon Div. Ft. Omaha, NE
Cadet Richard Furman '20	SMA Austin
Cadet James E. Gardner '19	Av. Sec. Call Field, Texas
Cadet Gabriel C. Harman '20	SMA Austin
Cadet Oral K. Jackson 'x15	SMA Austin
Cadet Richard M. Jarrell 'x14	SMA Austin
Cadet Roy Lawson 'x18	Aero. Sqdn. Selfridge Field, Michigan

Cadet William P. Mansker 'x17	SMA Austin
Cadet George L. Martin '20	SMA Austin
Cadet Melvin J. Miller '11	SMA Austin
Cadet John P. Read '20	SMA Austin
Cadet Francis H. Rust '19	SMA Austin
Cadet Walter N. Scott '20	SMA Austin
Cadet Harry H. Singleton '16	5th Aero. Sqdn. Ellington Field
Cadet Clyde Slay '16	ASSRC Taliaferro Field, Texas
Cadet John P. Shutt 'x15	SMA Austin
Cadet John F. Studer '20	SMA Austin
Cadet Ottis L. Taulman 'x18	Balloon Div. Ft. Omaha, NE
Cadet Louis T. Tighe '18	Av. Sec. Taliaferro Field
Cadet Joseph M. Tutner '15	Av. Sec. Ellington Field
Cadet Roy W. Voss '20	SMA Austin
Cadet Karl E. Wallace '21	ASSRC Kelly Field
Cadet Brecher Whaley 'x17	SMA Austin
Cadet Felix E. Whitely '18	ASSRC Call Field, Texas
Cadet Edgar F. Wilton 'x18	ASSRC Ellington Field
Cadet Hoy A. Woods '11	ASSRC Kelly Field
Cadet Frank L. Wotipka 'x15	SMA Austin

NOTES

Chapter 1

1. Sean McMeekin, *July 1914: Countdown to War*, New York: Basic Books, 2013, pp. 1–42; B. H. Liddell Hart, *The Real War 1914–1915*, New York: Back Bay Books, 1964, reprint, pp. 3–64.

2. Ruth McCawley, "American Attitudes Toward England and Germany as Reflected in Newspapers of Texas from 1914 to 1917." MA thesis, University of Texas, 1940; Ralph A. Wooster, *Texas and Texans in the Great War*. Buffalo Gap: State House Press, 2008, pp. 27–28.

3. David M. Kennedy, *Over Here: The First World War and American Society*, New York: Oxford University Press, 1980, pp. 5–48. See also Ross Gregory, *The Origins of American Intervention in the First World War*, New York: W. W. Norton & Company, 1971; Wooster, *Texas and Texans in the Great War*, p. 9.

4. Ray Stannard Baker, *Woodrow Wilson: Life and Papers – President 1913–1914*, New York: Charles Scribner, 1931, pp. 36–104.

5. John Dos Passos, *Mr. Wilson's War*, Garden City, NY: Doubleday & Company, 1962, pp. 87–128.

6. Baker, *Woodrow Wilson*, pp. 236–352; Larry Hill, *Emissaries to a Revolution*, Baton Rouge: Louisiana State University Press, 1973, pp. 7–10, 175; Michael C. Meyer, "The Arms of the *Ypriango*," *Hispanic American Historical Review*, August 1970, pp. 544–550; "Houston Boys at the Front," *Houston Chronicle*, May 3, 1914, and "Light Guardsmen at Hidalgo," *Houston Chronicle*, May 13, 1914. Note: Aggies included Harry L. Bennett, Jr. 'x14 and Henry DeWitt "Pancho Villa" Morse 'x14. Morse picked up the sobriquet after reportedly serving "several months" in General Villa's army in Mexico.

7. *Houston Post*, August 17, 1916, May 10, 1914; *Bryan Weekly Eagle*, May 18 and 25, 1916; *Brownsville Herald*, August 29, 1916; "Pancho Villa," *Houston Chronicle*, May 3, 1914. See also Frank E. Vandiver, *Blackjack Pershing*, 2 Vol., College Station: Texas A&M University Press, 1977, and Herbert M. Mason, Jr. *The Great Pursuit: General John J. Pershing's Punitive Expedition Across the Rio Grande to Destroy the Mexican Bandit Pancho Villa*. New York: Random House, 1970. Note: Two additional A&M cadets, Leander E. Ponder 'x17 of Bryan and Albert C. Schram 'x17 of Taylor, left the college in June 1916 after their junior year and

enlisted in the army on the Mexican border and were stationed at Oja de Agua in Company H, Second Texas Infantry.

8. John A. Adams, Jr. *The Vergara Affair*, College Station: Texas A&M University Press, 2017; Shakespeare, "Julius Caesar," Act 3, Scene 1, line 273. See also Gregory, *The Origins of American Intervention in the First World War*, 1971. Note: And in larger context, the lines of Marc Antony's speech:

> And Caesar's spirit, ranging for revenge,
> With Ate* by his side come hot from hell,
> Shall in these confines with a monarch's voice
> Cry Havoc and let slip the dogs of war.
> *Ate: Greek goddess of discord, folly, and vengeance

9. William C. Pool, " Military Aviation in Texas 1913–1917," *SWHQ*, April 1954, pp. 429–434; Maurer, ed., *The US Air Service in World War I*, Office of Air Force History, Washington, DC: GPO, 1978, Vol. II, pp. 19–22; Rebecca H. Cameron, *Training to Fly: Military Flight Training 1907–1945*. Washington, DC: GPO, 1999, pp. 9–10, 82; "Rebels to Have Aeroplanes," *The Sun* [New York], March 4, 1914.

10. Barbara W. Tuchman, *The Zimmermann Telegram*, New York: Ballantine, 1985, pp. 135–146; Will Englund, *March 1917*, New York: Norton, 2017, pp. 75–80.

11. Timothy J. Dunn, *The Militarization of the US-Mexico Border, 1978–1992: Low-Intensity Conflict Doctrine Comes Home*, Austin: CMAS Books, University of Texas, 1996, pp. 9–10.

12. "Aeroplanes to be Tried in Texas," *Bryan Daily Eagle*, May 14, 1909; Roger Bilstein and Jay Miller, *Aviation in Texas*, Austin: Texas Monthly Press, 1985, pp. 19–20; James J. Sloan, *Wings of Honor: American Airman in World War* I, Atglen, PA: Schiffer Publishing, 1994, 21, 404; John Adams, *Conflict and Commerce on the Rio Grande*, College Station: Texas A&M University Press, 2008, pp. 144–146; Lawson, *The First Air Campaign*, pp. 23–24. Note: For an excellent account of early Air Service operations in Texas see Gen. Ben D. Foulois's letter in Barney M. Giles, "Early Military Aviation in Texas," *SWHQ*, October 1950, pp. 143–150.

13. David L. Chapman, *Wings Over Aggieland*, College Station: Friends of the Sterling C. Evans Library, 1994; "It Will Fly Like a Bird: Impelled by Two Giant Wings," *Austin Statesman*, February 28, 1897, p. 14.

14. "Ross Volunteer Ball," *Bryan Daily Eagle*, April 22, 1911; "Ross Volunteers Give Annual Dance at A. & M." *Dallas Morning News*, April 24, 1911.

15. Chapman, *Wings Over Aggieland*, pp. 4–13; "The Elks-Moisant Aviation Engagement," *Bryan Daily Eagle*, May 22, 1912; *Longhorn 1913*, p. 290.

16. Samuel Hynes, *The Unsubstantial Air: American Fliers in the First World War*, New York: Farrar, Straus and Giroux, 2014, p. 4.

17. Interview with Henry C. Dethloff, July 19, 2016. See also J. Lecornu, Rene Terlet, trans. and Henry Dethloff, ed., *Aerial Navigation*, College Station: Intaglio Press, 2003; "The Airship," *Austin Daily Statesman*, April 19, 1897, and "The Airship," *Bryan Daily Eagle*, April 22, 1897.

18. Keith Jeffery, *1916: A Global History*, New York: Bloomsbury, 2015, pp. 314–325; Henry C. Dethloff, *Texas Aggies Go to War*, College Station: Texas A&M University Press, 2006, pp. 36, 229–230.

19. G. P. F. Jouine Collection, Cushing Library, Texas A&M University; "Jouine Receives His Sixth Wound," *Alumni Quarterly*, November 1918, p. 19; "Won French War Cross," *Alumni Quarterly*, May 1918, p. 18.

20. "Lt. Netherwood," *Evening Star*, December 12, 1913; Cameron, *Training to Fly*, pp. 82–86, 93–96; "Imperative Need of Training Airmen," *Boston Transcript*, reprinted in *Aerial Age Weekly*, June 28, 1915, p. 342; Juliette A. Hennessy, *The United States Air Arm, April 1861 to April 1917*, Washington, DC: GPO, 1985, p. 152.

21. "Netherwood and the Hupmobile," *Salt Lake Telegram*, July 11, 1915; Lawson, *The First Air Campaign*, p. 11; Phil Scott, *The Wrong Stuff: Attempts at Flight Before & After the Wright Brothers*, New York: Barnes and Noble, 2006, pp. 9–85. See also Roger D. Launis, "A New Way of War: The Development of Military Aviation in the West, 1908–1945," *Military History of the West*, Fall 1995, pp. 167–173. Note: The new "Aviation Section" was approved by the US Congress on July 18, 1914, in H.R. 5304 (Public Law 143).

22. "Airship Squad Flies to a Football Game," *The New York Times*, November 19, 1916; Marc Wortman, *The Millionaires Unit*, London; PAN Books, 2006, pp. 49–70; Hynes, *The Unsubstantial Air*, pp. 21–32.

23. Letter Cadet Harry B. Moses 'x18 to Dad, April 17, 1917, Harry B., Moses Papers, Briscoe American History Center, Austin; William B. Bizzell, "The Service of the College to the Nation," *Alumni Quarterly*, November 1917, pp. 3–6; "Prospects for College Appropriations," *Alumni Quarterly*, January 1917, p. 5; Dethloff, *Texas Aggies Go to War*, pp. 43–46.

24. "Texas 'Aggies' 1917 Southwest Champions," *Alumni Quarterly*, February 1918, pp. 3–4; John Adams, *Keepers of the Spirit*, College Station: Texas A&M University Press, 2001, pp. 86–88; Cameron, *Training to Fly*, pp. 93–105.

25. Hynes, *The Unsubstantial Air*, pp. 14–16; Gross, *American Military Aviation*, pp. 23–26.

26. "Value of Preparedness," *San Antonio Express*, May 17, 1917; Maurer, ed., *The US Air Service in World War I*, Vol. I, pp. 51, 93, 104; Vol. II, pp. 54, 75–87; Bruce N. Canfield, "Guns on the Border," *American Rifleman*, October 2016, pp. 60–67; Gross, *American Military Aviation*, pp. 25–29; A Friend, Fifty-First Annual Reunion of the Association of Graduates of the United States Military Academy, June 14, 1920, pp. 59–60.

27. "Abilene Col. Served Under Gen Billy Mitchell," *Abilene Reporter-News*, April 8, 1956; "Colonel Herbert Mason," *Brownwood Bulletin*, April 23, 1956.

28. "From San Antonio to Somme: Pershing Picked as Leader," *San Antonio Express*, May 19, 1917; "Pershing Men Must First be Trained in New Trench Warfare," *San Antonio Express*, May 20, 1917; Pool, "Military Aviation in Texas," *SWHQ*, pp. 443–54.

29. Leonard P. Ayers, *The War with Germany: A Statistical Summary*. Washington, DC: GPO, 1919, pp. 17–18; John J. Pershing, *My Experiences in the War*, vol. I, New York: Frederick A. Stokes, 1931, pp. 8–13.

30. Clarence Ousley, *History of the Agricultural and Mechanical College of Texas*, College Station: Bulletin, December 1, 1935, pp. 74–75; Edwin J. Kyle, "The Agricultural Graduate's Part in the War for Democracy," *Alumni Quarterly*, February 1918, pp. 10–11; "Military Tradition Dates Back to 1876," *Bryan Eagle*, October 3, 1950.

Chapter 2

1. "ROTC," *Annual Catalogue: A&M College of Texas*, College Station: A&M College, June 1, 1918, pp. 39–40; Officer Reserve Corps," *Alumni Quarterly*, January 1917, pp. 6–8; "Reserve Officer Training Corps on a New Basis," *Alumni Quarterly*, February 1919, pp. 7–8; Dethloff, *A Centennial History of Texas A&M, 1876–1976*, Vol. I, pp. 267–271; Gross, *American Military Aviation*, pp. 26–27. Note: The first four Aggies called to active duty and commissioned at Fort Leavenworth, Kansas, on November 30, 1916, were F. A. Roberts '13, FA; R. R. Allen '15, Cav.; P. W. Clarkson '15, 19th Inf.; and J. F. Ehlert '16, 32nd Inf. The general manager of the Southern Pacific Railroad, Edward B. Cushing '80, was recommended as a major in the engineering regiment and immediately assigned to foreign duty in France. Cushing, at 57 years old, was the oldest alumnus of Texas A&M on active duty in World War I.

2. John Payne, "David F. Houston's Presidency of Texas A. and M.," *SWHQ*, July 1954, pp. 22–35; *Austin Daily Statesman*, April 8, 1902; Ousley, *History of the Agricultural and Mechanical College*, pp. 60–65.

3. Dethloff, *Centennial History*, Vol. 1, pp. 217–230, 243–255, 264; Texas A&M, *Biennial Report, 1917–1918*, p. 22; Adams, *Keepers of the Spirit*, pp. 58–90; Link, *Woodrow Wilson and the Progressive Era, 1910–1917*, pp. 187–188.

4. Wooster, *Texas and Texans in the Great War*, pp. vii, 39, 168, fn13, 176. See also Walter L. Buenger, *The Path to a Modern South: Northern Texas between Reconstruction and the Great Depression*, Austin: University of Texas Press, 2001. Note: In addition to the early wave of Texans who volunteered for duty (both in the United States and Europe) in 1915–1916, by the fall of 1918 over 990,000 Texans had registered for the conscription or draft mandated by the US Congress. In Texas, selection of inductees was determined by local civilian board members, appointed by the president on the recommendation of the governor, on 279 draft boards.

5. Texas A&M *Biennial Report, 1915–16*, pp. 10–12; "Texas College Company," *Christian Science Monitor*, April 2, 1917, p. 3; Jerry Cooper and Henry C. Dethloff, *Footsteps*, College Station: Texas A&M University Press, 1991, pp. 64, 75, 116, 152.

6. William P. Ayers, "The Service of the College to the Nation," *Alumni Quarterly*, November 1917, pp. 3–6; "General Pershing Praises the American Farmer, *Alumni Quarterly*, February 1917, p. 23.

7. Minutes of the Texas A&M Board of Directors, March 23, 1917, III, pp. 212–213; Charles W. Crawford, *One Hundred Years of Engineering at Texas A&M 1876–1976*, College Station: Privately Published, 1976, 40–41; W. B. Bizzell, "The Service of the College to the Nation," *Alumni Quarterly*, November 1917, p. 4; Bizzell, "The Service Ideal of the College," *Battalion*, October 31, 1917; Barbara Donalson, *Kyle Tough*, Bryan: The Oaks Press, 2003, pp. 121–122.

8. Letter Cadet Harry Moses to Dad, April 17, 24, 1917, Moses Papers; "Reserve Officers' Camp Is Opened at Leon Springs, 1,169 Men Registered First Day," *San Antonio Express*, May 9, 1917; *Bryan Eagle*, May 4, 18, 1917, and June 2, 1917; Annual Report of the A&M College, 1919–1920, p. 3; Adams, *Keepers of the Spirit*, pp. 90–100.

9. "Seventy-Three in Uniform Given Their Diplomas as A&M Breaks Precedent," *San Antonio Express News*, June 3 and 4, 1917; "Army Takes Eight of A. & M. Staff," *Bryan Eagle*, October 4, 1917; "Commencement Exercise Cancelled," *Alumni Quarterly*, May 1917, pp. 10–12; "Leon Springs," *Alumni Quarterly*, pp. 4–5; Letter Cadet Harry Moses to Dad, November 11, 1917, Moses Papers; Dethloff, *Centennial History*, Vol. I, pp. 269–263. Note: The first ROTC training began at Texas A&M in September 1917, yet did not begin in earnest until early 1919. The long-held myth of the graduation under "a big oak tree" at Camp Funston is part of Aggie lore; in fact, the ceremonies took place in the recently completed YMCA auditorium at the camp. Departing A&M College faculty and staff included the following:

Ike Ashburn, Public Relations
Charles L. Beatty, Dir. Ag. Exten.
B. O. Bethel. Vet. Med.
Dana X. Bible, Coach
O. Brown, Asst. Prof. Horticulture
O. F. Chastain, Prof. History
B. K. Coghlan, Asst. Prof. Engineering
Otto Ehlinger, Physician
Aubrey Finley, Janitor
Darden Ford, Dir. of Music
G. W. Hanson, Mech. Eng.
Maurice Hayes, Entomologist
J. H. Lowe, Asst. Prof. Biology
Thomas F. Mayo, Prof. English
W. G. McGee, Ag. Extension
E. E. McQuillen '20, coach
Tyra Jane Morgan, Clerk
R. L. Morrison, Prof. Eng.
Phillip Nero, Janitor
Clarence Ousley, Ag. Extension
LeRoy Rhodes, Prof. Ag. Eng.
Verne A. Scott '14, Vet. Med.
Frank J. Skeeler '10, Inst. Physics
W. L. Stangel '15, Asst Prof. An. Hus.

C. C. Whitney, Asst. Prof. Vet. Med.
A. B. Wilcox, Accountant
W. Wipperman, Asst. Prof. M.E.

10. Charles Puryear, "The War and the College," *Alumni Quarterly*, November 1918, pp. 3–4; "Reorganization of the College Program," *A&M Bulletin*, December 15, 1918, pp. 4–8; Woodrow Wilson, "Message: Students' Army Training Corps," *SamSun* [Austin], October 5, 1918; "College Students in Special Corps," *San Antonio Express*, October 3, 1918; Adams, *Keepers of the Spirit*, pp. 95–98. Note: The first official notification to Texas A&M of the SATC training was on August 15, 1918.

11. "War Work at College," *Alumni Quarterly*, April 1918, pp. 4–5; "Prof. F. C. Bolton," *Bryan Daily Eagle*, April 16, 1918; *Twenty-First Biennial Report of the Agricultural and Mechanical College of Texas*, College Station: Bulletin, October 15, 1918, pp. 22–24; J. C. Nagle, "War Training Activities at the Agricultural and Mechanical College of Texas," *Proceedings of the Twenty-Sixth Annual Meeting*, 1918, pp. 63–77. Note: Texas A&M offered the only comprehensive meteorology program in the nation, training over 1,000 weather observers. See *San Antonio Express*, July 21, 1918, October 12, 1918, and Charles F. Brooks, "Collegiate Instruction in Meteorology," *Monthly Weather Review*, No. 12, 1918, pp. 555–560.

12. Charles Puryear, "The War and the College," *Alumni Quarterly*, November 1918, pp. 3–4; "Mechanics for Pershing's Army," *Dallas Morning* News, January 20, 1918; "600 More Soldiers Ordered to A. and M. College," *Bryan Eagle*, May 2, 1918; "700 Men Arrive College Station for Auto-Mechanics Course," *Bryan Eagle*, June 17, 1918; Crawford, *One Hundred Years*, pp. 42–43; *Bryan Eagle*, April 4, 10, 1918, and September 29, 1918; *Houston Post*, April 8, 1918; Adams, *Keepers of the Spirit*, pp. 90–95.

13."Honor War Certificates," *Bryan Daily Eagle*, May 28, 1918; "A&M Will Be Training Camp," *Alumni Quarterly*, February 1918, pp. 21–22; "Battalion Suspended," *Alumni Quarterly*, November 1918, p. 12; "Prexy Inaugurates Voluntary Chapel," *Battalion*, April 24, 1918; Crawford, *Engineering at Texas A&M*, p. 43; Texas A&M *Longhorn* (1919), p. 113; Dethloff, *Centennial History*, I, pp. 276–271; *Houston Post*, April 15, 1918.

14. Henry Dethloff and Stephen Searcy, *Engineering Agriculture at Texas A&M: The First Hundred Years*, College Station: Texas A&M University Press, 2015, p. 20; *Abilene Daily Reporter*, May 2, 1918; Chapman, *Wings Over Aggieland*, pp. 16–17. Note: Landings were also made at Dellwood Park north of campus and at the small field in Bryan. The Pavilion had 20,000 square feet of open floor space.

15. "Airplanes Wrecked at A. and M. College But Nobody Injured," *Bryan Daily Eagle*, April 6, 19, 23, 1918; "Flying Is Becoming Safer, Say Veteran Field Instructors," *Galveston Daily News*, September 1, 1918, and "Liberty Airplanes are Built to Fight," *Galveston Daily News*, September 17, 1918; *Longhorn*, 1919, p. 272; Chapman, *Wings Over Aggieland*, pp. 8–9.

16. "Additional Interurban Service," *Reveille*, November 7, 1918; *Bryan Daily Eagle* April 1, 4, 1918.

17. E. B. Cushing Papers, Cushing Library, College Station, Texas; W. M. Baines, ed. *Houston's Part in the World War*, Houston, 1919, p. 83; "Former A. and M. Man [Cushing] Decorated by Marshall of France," *Bryan Daily Eagle*, June 17, 1919; "The 'OO LA LA' Times Features Col. Cushing and Major Hutson," *Alumni Quarterly*, February 1919, p. 22; "Colonel Cushing Decorated with French Legion of Honor," *Alumni Quarterly*, November 1919, p. 26.

18. "Students of A. and M. to Enter Training Schools," *Galveston Daily News*, October 7, 1918; Gross, *American Military Aviation*, pp. 26–35; Hynes, *The Unsubstantial Air*, pp. 64–82; Lawson, *The First Air Campaign*, pp. 34–42.

Chapter 3

1. Cooke, *The US Air Service in the Great War*, pp. 1–5: Cameron, *Training to Fly*, pp. 107–128; David McCullough, *The Wright Brothers*, pp. 17–80; H. G. Wells, *The War in the Air*, New York: Boni and Liveright, Inc., 1917; Gross, *American Military Aviation*, pp. 12–15; John Morrow, *The Great War in the Air: Military Aviation from 1909-1921*, Washington, DC: Smithsonian Institute Press, 1993, pp. 32–87. Note: Wells's fictional look at flying was published a mere 40 months after the first flight at Kitty Hawk. It was written in 1907 and first published in serial form in 1908, and then as a book in the fall of 1908.

2. Daso, *Hap Arnold*, p. 63; Gross, *American Military Aviation*, pp. 17–20; Cameron, *Training to Fly*, pp. 72–80. See also Alfred T. Mahan, *Influence of Sea Power upon History 1670–1783*, Boston: Little Brown, 1890.

3. R. Borlase Matthews, *The Aviation Pocket Book for 1917*, London: Crosby Lockwood and Son, 5th edition, 1917, pp. title page and xviii. Note: Matthews first published his compendium of aviation data, formulas, industry assessments, and principles of flight in 1913. Two key items in his books are that he gives the full credit for manned flight to the Wright brothers, and second, he accurately predicts in 1917 that, "today a flight across the Atlantic is a practical possibility," predating Charles Lindbergh's solo trans-Atlantic feat in 1927 and stating that "the feat will lie in abeyance until peace once more reigns supreme" with the end of the war. Another telling fact on the advancement of American aviation is that France and England combined published 12 major aviation periodicals, and the United States only one—*Aeronautics*—which took a lot of content from its agent in London. See also Dan Hampton, *The Flight: Charles Lindbergh's Daring and Immortal 1927 Transatlantic Crossing*, New York: Harper Collins, 2017.

4. Giles, "Early Military Aviation Activities in Texas," p. 151; Lucian H. Thayer, *America's First Eagles: History of the US Air Service*, San Jose: James Bender Publishing, 1983, p. 9; Gross, *American Military Aviation*, pp. 28–30.

5. Thayer, *America's First Eagles*, pp. 30–33; Douglas V. Smith, ed. *One Hundred Years of US Navy Air Power*, Annapolis: Naval Institute Press, 2010, pp. 2–8. Note: In August 1914, America, the birthplace of powered flight, had a mere 23 military airplanes.

6. "War Office and Aviation," *London Times*, February 19, 1914. See also "War Airships Drive Reach 250 Miles an Hour," *San Antonio Express*, May 10, 1917.

7. Daso, *Hap Arnold*, pp. 44–50; Lawson, *The First Air Campaign*, pp. 106–109; William Head, *Every Inch a Soldier*, College Station: Texas A&M University Press, 1995, pp. 50–54; Kennett, *The First Air War*, pp. 119–125; Cameron, *Training to Fly*, pp. 59–70; Giles, "Early Military Aviation in Texas, *SWHQ*, pp. 145–146; John F. Ross, *Enduring Courage*, New York: St. Martin's Griffin, 2014, p. xviii. Note: Lt. Hap Arnold earned his wings at the Wright Aviation School in Dayton, Ohio, after 38 flights totaling a mere 3 hours and 48 minutes of flight time.

8. Letter Cadet Harry Moses to "Muz," October 1, 1917, Moses Papers.

9. "Reserve Officers' Camp Is Opened at Leon Springs, 1,169 Men Registered First Day," *San Antonio Express*, May 9, 1917; Lawson, *The First Air Campaign*, pp. 33–35.

10. "Texas University Aviation School to Turn Out 200 Graduates in Flying," *San Antonio Express*, June 3, 1917; "Ground School at A. & M. and Air School at Austin," *Dallas Morning News*, June 24, 1918; "Ground Officers Finishing Training," *San Antonio Express News*, November 9, 1917; Hiram Bingham, *An Explorer in the Air Service*, New Haven: Yale University Press, 1920, pp. 43–44; Hynes, *The Unsubstantial Air*, pp. 46–52. See also J'Nell L. Pate, *Arsenal of Defense: Ft. Worth Military Legacy*, Denton: Texas State Historical Association, 2011, pp. 20–39, and Kenneth B. Ragsdale, *Austin, Cleared for Takeoff*, Austin: University of Texas Press, 2004, pp. 28–43.

11. Gross, *American Military Aviation*, pp. 38–39.

12. "The Right Stuff," *Daily Telegram* [Temple], June 24, 1918.

13. "Texas Responds Nobly to Call for an Increased Production," *Galveston Daily News*, September 15, 1918; Lawson, *The First Air Campaign*, p. 155; Cameron, *Training to Fly*, pp. 107–145.

14. "De Havillands Doing Well," *The New York Times*, October 2, 1918; Thayer, *America's First Eagles*, p. 88; Cameron, *Training to Fly*, pp. 107–108, 147–160; Gross, *American Military Aviation*, pp. 40–44.

15. John H. Barry, *The Great Influenza: The Story of the Deadliest Pandemic in History*, New York: Penguin Books, 2004, pp. 176–193; Interview with Winnie Adams Sims, December 23, 1984.

16. *Bryan Daily Eagle*, September 30, 1918; "Uncle Sam's Advice on Flu," October 18, 1918; and "Spanish Influenza" October 2, 1918; Barry, *Influenza*, pp. 181, 224, 307, 340, 404. Note: The medical challenge was determining the true nature of the illness and how to most effectively treat it. The 1918 epidemic associated with "influenza" spawned a secondary, direct connection with viral pneumonias acute respiratory distress syndrome.

17. *Bryan Daily Eagle*, September 30, 1918.

18. *Bryan Daily Eagle*, October 2, 3, 4, 1918: "Football for 1918," *Alumni Quarterly*, November 1918, p. 5; *Longhorn*, 1919, p. 152; Barry, *Influenza*, pp. 208, 307.

19. "Quarter of Million Men Will Be Sent to France Each Month," *The New York Times*, October 15, 1918; *Bryan Daily Eagle*, October 5, 1918; Barry, *Influenza*, pp. 224, 232, 312, 319.

20. "Deplorable College Conditions Condemned by Defense Council," *Bryan Daily Eagle*, October 10, 1918; "Barracks Five," *Bryan Daily Eagle*, October

11, 1918; "Seven More Dead in 48 Hour College Death Toll," *Bryan Daily Eagle*, October 14, 1918; "She's Still Known as Mom by Thousands of Aggie Exes," *Battalion*, January 5, 1966.

21. Interview with Charles Crawford March 30, 1971, as seen in Dethloff, *Centennial History*, Vol. I, p. 280. See also T. F. Wiesen Interview, August 1, 1974, p. 10, Cushing Archives.

22. "Conditions Are Better," *Bryan Daily Eagle*, October 15, 1918; "Two More Soldiers Die at College; Situation Better," *Bryan Daily Eagle*, October 17, 1918; "Commercial Club Passes Resolution Concerning A. &. M.," *Bryan Daily Eagle*, October 22, 1918; "Music Director of A. and M. College Dies at Hospital," *Bryan Daily Eagle*, October 23, 1918.

23. "The A. and M. Regiment Is Ready for Federalization," *Alumni Quarterly*, November 1918, p. 10; "Nine Men Appointed Infantry Captains," *Dallas Morning News*, July 12, 1918.

24. Hoehling, *The Great Epidemic*, 1961, p. 62; Alfred W. Crosby, *America's Forgotten Pandemic*, 1989, pp. 56–87, 314; "Spanish Influenza Spreading in U.S.," *Washington Post*, September 16, 1918.

25. Crosby, *Pandemic*, p. 86; Wortman, *The Millionaires' Unit*, p. 224. See also Jeremy Brown, *Influenza*, New York: Atria Books, 2018.

Chapter 4

1. Henry Wolff, "Aviator Flew Skies Over France," *Victoria Advocate*, November 20, 1988.

2. Cooke, *The US Air Service in the Great War*, pp. 1–3; Lawson, *The First Air Campaign*, pp. 11, 31–34, 42–44; "The Future of the Submarine War," *Bryan Daily Eagle*, October 19, 1918; Fitzsimons, *War Planes and Air Battles*, p. 4.

3. Letters Henry Moses to Tad, November 30, 1917, and Moses to "Muz" and Dad, February 18, 1918, Moses Papers.

4. Letters Lt. Moses to C.O. 8th A.I.C., June 2, 1918, and Dayton Moses to Army Adjutant General, July 20, 1918, Moses Papers.

5. Thomas H. Greer, *The Development of Air Doctrine in Army Air Arm 1917–1941*, Washington, DC: GPO, 1985, pp. 3–11; Gross, *American Military Aviation*, pp. 40–41; Lawson, *The First Air Campaign*, p. 39.

6. Lee Kennett, *The First Air War, 1914–1918*, New York: The Free Press, 1991, p. 129.

7. David Chapman, "Jesse Easterwood '09: WWI Hero and Pioneer in Naval Aviation," *Texas Aggie*, June 1994.

8. "Passing of a Hero," *Wills Point Chronicle*, June 11, 1919; Sloan, *Wings of Honor*, p. 281: Maurer, ed. *US Air Service*, pp. 103–104.

9. College Station, *Longhorn*, 1910, p. 172, and *Longhorn*, 1911, p. 160; *San Antonio Express*, September 13, 1918.

10. *El Paso Herald*, August 31, 1918; September 3, 1918.

11. *El Paso Herald*, September 3, 1918; http://valor.militarytimes.com/recipientid

12. "Aerial Observation," *SamSun* [Austin], November 2, 1918; Lee Kennett,

The First Air War 1914–1918. New York: The Free Press, 1991, pp. 39–41; Eric and Jane Lawson, *The First Air Campaign 1914–1918*, Conshohocken, PA: Combined Books, 1996, p. 59.

13. "Captain Trickey Has A Narrow Escape," *Alumni Quarterly*, November 1918, p. 11; Sloan, *Wings of Honor*, p. 160; "Trickey, Local Boy Rides to Safety on Wing of Plane," *Bryan Daily Eagle*, October 2, 1918.

14. *Congressional Record*, Vol. 1484, No. 134, October 11, 2002, p. E1852; Sloan, *Wings of Honor*, pp. 325–326; "Death of Lt. George R. Phillips," *US Air Service*, March 1920, p. 36; Daniel P. Morse, *The History of the 50th Aero Squadron*, 1990, pp. 57–58. Note: Lt. Phillips was killed in an airplane crash at McAllen, Texas, when a wing malfunctioned in January 1920.

15. "Martin Carl Giesecke," *The Longhorn 1912*, p. 98; Sloan, *Wings of Honor*, pp. 229–230; *San Antonio Express*, September 18, 1917; Frederick M. Clapp, *A History of the 17th Aero Squadron*, December 1918, reprint by Nashville: The Battery Press, 1990, pp. 9–13.

16. Clapp, *A History of the 17th Aero Squadron*, pp. 106–142.

17. Sloan, *Wings of Honor*, pp. 236–237; *Kerrville Mountain Sun*, December 22, 1979; "Iron Crosses Mark Spots Where Airplanes Are Hit," *Bryan Daily Eagle*, October 23, 1918.

18. *Dallas Morning News*, February 6, 1918; June 15, 1919; March 6, 1971; *Brownwood Bulletin*, October 17, 1919; Sloan, *Wings of Honor*, p. 366.

19. "Earle Graham," *Bryan Daily Eagle*, May 31, 1917; Cyrus Earle Graham Draft Card, May 29, 1917, Brazos County Records; "Graham Tells Story of Half Mile Fall," *Austin Statesman*, August 8, 1918.

20. *Alumni Quarterly*, November 1918, p. 13 and February 1919, p. 4; *Bryan Daily Eagle*, August 8, 1918; *Austin Statesman*, August 8, 1918; "Body of A&M Man Arrived From France," *Battalion*, November 20, 1920.

21. Lawson, *The First Air Campaign*, pp. 159–169.

22. Interview with Mrs. Marilyn Routt-Thomson. Note: The father of Joe E. Routt '37, Joseph L. Routt 'x16, was a veteran of World War I, and his grandfather, J. R. Routt, was a member of the Class of 1888.

23. Tim Cohane, *Great College Football Coaches of the Twenties and Thirties*, New Rochelle: Arlington House, 1973, pp. 25–29; Brazos County Records, Dana X. Bible Draft Registration Card, n.d., n.p.

24. "Coach Bible Back," *Alumni Quarterly*, May 1919, p. 14; "D. X. Bible," *Alumni Quarterly*, August 1918, p. 26; Letter Lt. Harry Moses to Dad, January 13, 1918, Moses Papers; Clarence G. Barth, *History of the Twentieth Aero Squadron*, Nashville: The Battery Press, reprint in 1990 of 1920 edition, pp. 50–51.

25. "Concerning the Death of Lieut. Robert Thompson," *Temple Daily Telegram*, October 20, 1918; "Man of '18 Class Tells of France and Flying," *The Megaphone* [Georgetown, Texas], October 22, 1918; "Hun Ship Downed by Texas Flier," *Beaumont Enterprise*, October 22, 1918; Sloan, *Wings of Honor*, pp. 244, 248.

26. "For Hal from Mother." Hal Greer Papers, Daughters of the Texas Revolution, Alamo, San Antonio. See also Hal Greer to My Dear Mother, October 16,

1918, and Mrs. Hal W. Greer to S. Terry Brown, February 17, 1936, seen in Greer Papers.

27. *Bryan Weekly Eagle*, May 30, 1918; "75,000 College Men in Our Service," *The New York Times*, July 14, 1918; Colonel Clarence Ousley Secretary of Agriculture," *Alumni Quarterly*, February 1918, p. 12; "Texas Leads in Percent of Alumni in the Service," *Alumni Quarterly*, August 1918, p. 10; "A. and M. Man Praised by President Wilson," *Alumni Quarterly*, November 1919, p. 12; "Texas A. & M. Ranks Second in Number of Men in Service," *Fort Worth Star Telegram*, July 20, 1918. Note: At times, the calculations of the exact number of "A&M men" seem in conflict due to frequent confusion between the accounting for A&M "graduates," sometimes referred to as alumni, and "former" or ex-students who had not completed their requirements for a formal degree prior to being inducted in the military.

28. "Hugh McFarland Cited by French for His Heroic Service," *Alumni Quarterly*, May 1919, p. 15; "Captain Buchanan Awarded Croix de Guerre," *Alumni Quarterly*, February 1919, p. 11; "Jouine Receives his Sixth Wound," and "Major Ike Ashburn Gassed and Sniped," *Alumni Quarterly*, November 1918, p. 19. Note: The Silver Star award for gallantry was a small "device" added to the campaign medal; later, the Silver Star Medal was created to replace the device.

Chapter 5

1. Ousley, *History of the Agricultural and Mechanical College of Texas*, p. 74; Bill Page, "Gold Star Aggies of World War I," 2016, Evans Library, College Station.

2. "De Havilland Planes and Liberty Motors Popular," *Dallas Morning News*, October 2, 1918; "Col. House in France on Peace Mission," *Dallas Morning News*, October 25, 1918; "Armistice and Unconditional Surrender," *Dallas Morning News*, October 7, 1918: "Aircraft Investigations Report Sent to Wilson With Recommendations, *Galveston Daily News*, November 1, 1918.

3. "The A. and M. Spirit Follows," *Alumni Quarterly*, February 1919, p. 13.

4. "College War Record," *Alumni Quarterly*, November 1919, p. 19.

5. Annual Report of the A&M College, 1919–1920, p. 22.

6. Cooper and Dethloff, Walking Tour; "Memorial Stadium," *Alumni Quarterly*, February 1920, pp. 2–3, 13–147.

7. *Houston Post*, June 17, 1919, p. 5.

BIBLIOGRAPHY

Government Documents

Ayers, Leonard. *The War With Germany: A Statistical Summary*. Washington, DC: GPO, 1919.

Bureau of the Census. *Mortality Statistics, 1918*. Washington, DC: GPO, 1920.

Handbook of Federal World War [One] Agencies and Their Records: 1917–1921. National Archives. Washington, DC: GPO, 1943.

United States Army. *Order of Battle of the United States Land Forces in the World War*. 3 vols. Washington, DC: Center of Military History, 1938.

United States Army. "Report of the Chief of Air Service." In *United States Army in World War, 1917–1919*. 17 vols. Washington, DC: Center of Military History, 1989, 225–290.

United States Army. *United States Army in World War, 1917–1919*. 17 vols. Washington, DC: Center of Military History, 1989.

United States Congress. *Congressional Record, 65th Congress*. Washington, DC: GPO, 1917–1919.

Primary

Annual Catalogue: A&M College of Texas. 1916–1920.

A&M Alumni Quarterly. College Station, 1916–1920.

Brooks, Arthur R. "A History of the 22nd Aero Squadron, 'Shooting Stars.'" *Cross and Cockade*, Summer 1963, pp. 106–136.

Bryant, J. M. "History of the School of Military Aeronautics." Unpublished manuscript, T. S. Painter Papers, Briscoe Center for American History, University of Texas, Austin.

Class of 1913: Historical Directory and Biography 1909–1913. College Station: Association of Former Students, 1953.

Directory of Former Students of the Agricultural and Mechanical College of Texas. College Station: Association Former Students, 1938.

Edward B. Cushing Papers, Cushing Library, Texas A&M.

"Gold Book: A&M College of Texas." College Station: *Alumni Quarterly*, August 1919.

Hal Irby Greer Papers, Daughters of the Republic of Texas Library, San Antonio.

Harry Bowman Moses Papers. Briscoe Center for American History, Austin.

Higham, Robin. *100 Years of Air Power & Aviation*. College Station: Texas A&M University Press, 2003.

Interview of T. E. Wiesen by Charles Schultz, August 1, 1974, Cushing Library.

Interview with David McCullough, "The Wright Brothers." Book TV, C-SPAN2, September 5, 2015.

Jesse L. Easterwood Papers, Cushing Library G. P. F. Jouine Collection, Cushing Library, Texas A&M University.

Longhorn. College Station: Texas A&M, 1903–1922.

Minutes of the Board of Directors, A&M College of Texas. College Station, 1916–1919.

Moses, Harry B. "LaGuardia's Cadets in Italy." Unpublished manuscript, c. 1950, Moses Papers.

Muster Roll of Officers and Enlisted Men of the US Marine Corps, Port Royal, S.C., May 31, 1931. Ancestry.com

Page '76, Bill, ed. "When Aggieland Turned Khaki: World War I at Texas A&M." College Station, July 25, 2016.

Pershing, John J. *My Experiences in the War*. New York: Frederick A. Stokes, 1931.

Texas War Records. Briscoe Center of American History, Austin.

US Congress. *Congressional Record*. Vol. 1484, No. 134, October 11, 2002, p. E1852.

US Congress. House. "Myron J. Conway and Others." 69th Congress, 1st session, Report No. 808, April 9, 1926.

World War I: Aggies in Service Papers, Cushing Library, Texas A&M University.

World War I: Spanish Influenza Epidemic Papers, Cushing Library.

US Justice Department. "World War I Casualty and Death Tables." Washington, DC: USJD.gov.

Secondary

Adams, John A. *Conflict and Commerce on the Rio Grande*. College Station: Texas A&M University Press, 2008.

Adams, John A. *Keepers of the Spirit*. College Station: Texas A&M University Press, 2001.

Adams, John A. *Murder and Intrigue on the Mexican Border: Governor Colquitt, President Wilson, and the Vergara Affair*. College Station: Texas A&M University Press, 2018.

Adams, John A. *We Are The Aggies*. College Station: Texas A&M University Press, 1978.

Ballard, Jack S. *War Bird Ace*. College Station: Texas A&M University Press, 2007.

Barth, Clarence G. *History of the Twentieth Aero Squadron*. Nashville, TN: Battery Press, 1990 (reprint of 1920 edition).

Bates, Charles C., and John F. Fuller. *America's Weather Warriors 1814–1985*. College Station: Texas A&M University Press, 1986.

Baxley, Michelle. "The Year That Changed American and Texas: The Great Influenza Epidemic of 1918." *Touchstone* 21, 2001, pp. 35–43.

Biddle, Charles. *The Way of the Eagle.* New York: Charles Scribner's Sons, 1919.

Bilstein, Roger, and Jay Miller. *Aviation in Texas.* Austin: Texas Monthly Press, 1985.

Bingham, Hiram. *An Explorer in the Air Service.* New Haven, CT: Yale University Press, 1920.

Bishop, William A. *Winged Warfare.* New York: Arco Publishing, 1981.

Bleakley, Bruce A. *Dallas Aviation.* Charleston, SC: Arcadia Publishing, 2011.

Brooks, Charles F. "Collegiate Instruction in Meteorology." *Monthly Weather Review*, No. 12, 1918, pp. 555–560.

Brundidge, Glenna F. *Brazos County History: Rich Past—Bright Future.* Bryan, TX: Family History Foundation, 1986.

Cameron, Rebecca H. *Training to Fly: Military Flight Training 1907–1945.* Washington, DC: GPO, 1999.

Canfield, Bruse N., "Guns on the Border." *American Rifleman*, October 2016, pp. 60–67.

Chapman, David L. *Wings Over Aggieland.* College Station: Friends of the Sterling C. Evans Library, 1994.

Clapp, Frederick M. *A History of the 17th Aero Squadron.* Nashville, TN: Battery Press, 1990 (reprint of 1918 edition).

Cole, Christopher, ed. *Royal Flying Corps 1915–1916.* Chatham, MA: W. & J. Mackey Co., 1969.

Cooke, James J. *The US Air Service in the Great War, 1917–1919.* Westport, CT: Praeger, 1996.

Copper, Jerry, and Henry Dethloff. *Footsteps: A Guided Tour of the Texas A&M University Campus.* College Station: Texas A&M University Press, 1991.

Corn, Joseph J. *The Winged Gospel: America's Romance with Aviation, 1900–1950.* New York: Oxford University Press, 1983.

Courtwright, David T. *Sky as Frontier: Adventure, Aviation, and Empire.* College Station: Texas A&M University Press, 2005.

Cox, Patricia L. "'An Enemy Closer to Us Than Any European Power': The Impact of Mexican Texan Public Opinion before World War I." *SWHQ*, July 2001, pp. 41–80.

Crawford, Charles W. *One Hundred Years of Engineering at Texas A&M, 1876–1976.* College Station: Privately Published, 1976.

Crosby, Alfred W. *America's Forgotten Pandemic: The Influenza of 1918.* Cambridge, UK: Cambridge University Press, 1989.

Daso, Dik A. *Hap Arnold and the Evolution of American Airpower.* Washington, DC: Smithsonian Institute Press, 2000.

Delve, Ken. *World War One in the Air.* Ramsbury, UK: Crowood Press, 1997.

Dethloff, Henry C. *A Centennial History of Texas A&M University 1876–1976.* 2 Vols. College Station: Texas A&M University Press, 1975.

Dethloff, Henry C. *Texas Aggies Go To War.* College Station: Texas A&M University Press, 2006.

Dethloff, Henry C., and Stephen Searcy. *Engineering Agriculture at Texas A&M: The First Hundred Years.* College Station: Texas A&M University Press, 2015.

Donalson, Barbara. *Kyle Tough.* Bryan, TX: The Oaks Press, 2003.

Eddins, Rufus R., and Herbert R. Voelcker, eds. *Class of 1909: Life at A&M as We Knew It 1905–1909.* College Station: 1966.

Eliot, Charles W., foreword. *Harper's Pictorial Library of the World War.* New York: Harper and Brother Publishers, 1920.

Fitzsimons, Bernard, ed. *War Planes and Air Battles of World War I.* Sidney: Ure Smith, 1973.

Flammer, Philip M. *A Vivid Air: The Lafayette Escadrille.* Athens: University of Georgia Press, 1981.

Flood, Charles B. *First to Fly: The Story of the Lafayette Escadrille.* New York: Atlantic Monthly Press, 2015.

Foulois, MajGen Benjamin D. " . . . and Teach Yourself to Fly." *Reader's Digest,* October 1960, pp. 50–54.

Frandsen, Bert. *Hat in the Ring: The Birth of American Air Power in the Great War.* Washington, DC: Smithsonian Books, 2003.

Giles, Barney M. "Early Military Aviation Activities in Texas." *SWHQ,* October 1950, pp. 143–158.

Glynn, Gary. "1st Aero Squadron in Pursuit of Pancho Villa." *American Legion Magazine,* November 1997, pp. 50–56.

Greer, Thomas H. *The Development of Air Doctrine in the Army Air Arm 1917–1941.* Washington, DC: 1985.

Gregory, Ross. *The Origins of Americas Intervention in the First World War.* New York: W. W. Norton & Company, 1971.

Gross, Charles J. *American Military Aviation.* College Station: Texas A&M University Press, 2006.

Hart, B. H. Liddell. *The Real War 1914–1918.* New York: Back Bay Books, 1964 (reprint).

Hart, Percival G. *History of the135th Aero Squadron.* Nashville, TN: Battery Press, 1990 (reprint of 1939 edition).

Haslett, Elmer. *Luck of the Wing.* New York: E. P. Dutton, 1920.

Hays, Robert E. Jr. "Military Aviation in Texas, 1917–1919." *Texas Military History,* Spring 1983, pp. 1–13.

Head, William. *Every Inch a Soldier.* College Station: Texas A&M University Press, 1995.

Hennessy, Juliette A. *The United States Army Air Arm.* Washington, DC: GPO, 1985.

Hoehling, A. A. *The Great Epidemic.* Boston: Little, Brown and Company, 1961.

Hynes, Samuel. *The Unsubstantial Air: American Fliers in the First World War.* New York: Farrar, Straus and Giroux, 2014.

Launis, Roger D. "A New Way of War: The Development of Military Aviation in the American West, 1908–1945." *Military History of the West,* Fall 1995, pp. 167–173.

Jeffry, Keith. *1916: Global History.* New York: Bloomsbury, 2015.

Johnson, Edward C. *Marine Corps Aviation: The Early Years 1912–1940*. Washington, DC: USMC/GPO, 1977.

Johnson, Pamela W. *The Corps: The Core of A&M*. College Station: Privately Printed, 2005.

Kennedy, David M. *Over Here: The First World War and America Society*. New York: Oxford University Press, 1980.

Kennett, Lee. *The First Air War 1914–1918*. New York: The Free Press, 1991.

Larson, Paul L., K. I. Burge, and K. L. Barr. *The First Wings of War: Air Force Reserve in World War I*. Robins ABF: HQAFB, 2015.

Lawson, Eric, and Jane Lawson. *The First Air Campaign—1914–1918*. Conshohocken, PA: Combined Books, 1996.

Leach, Norman S. *Cavalry of the Air*. Toronto: Dundurn, 2014.

Lebow, Eileen F. *Cal Rodgers and the Vin Fiz: The First Transcontinental Flight*. Washington, DC: Smithsonian Institute Press, 1989.

Lecornu, J., and Henry Dethloff, eds. *Aerial Navigation—1903*. College Station: Intaglio Press, 2003.

Literary Digest, June 8, 1918.

Mahan, Alfred T. *Influence of Sea Power upon History 1670–1783*. Boston: Little Brown, 1890.

Mann, C. R. "The Effect of the War on Engineering Education." *Engineering Education Bulletin*, November 1, 1917, pp. 108–118.

Maurer, Maurer, ed. *The US Air Service in World War I*. 4 Vol. Office of Air Force History. Washington, DC: GPO, 1978.

McConnell, James R. *Flying for France*. Garden City, NY: Doubleday, Page, 1917.

McCullough, David. *The Wright Brothers*. New York: Simon & Schuster, 2015.

McKibben, Frank P. "The Colleges and the War." *Engineering Education Bulletin*, May 1919, pp. 363–388.

McMeekin, Sean. *July 1914: Countdown to War*. New York: Basic Books, 2013.

Mitchell, William. *Memoirs of World War I*. New York: Random House, 1960.

Morrow, John. *The Great War in the Air: Military Aviation from 1909–1921*. Washington, DC: Smithsonian Institute Press, 1993, pp. 32–87.

Morse, Daniel P. *The History of the 50th Aero Squadron*. Nashville, TN: Battery Press, 1990.

O'Sullivan, Kevin M. *The Great War: A World War I Exhibit Featuring the Aggie Experience*. College Station: Cushing Library, 2015.

Ousley, Clarence. *History of the Agricultural and Mechanical College of Texas*. College Station: Bulletin, December 1, 1935.

Pate, J'Nell L. *Arsenal of Defense: Fort Worth's Military Legacy*. Denton: Texas State Historical Association, 2011.

Patrick, Jeff. *Guarding the Border*. College Station: Texas A&M University Press, 2009.

Payne, John. "David F. Houston's Presidency of Texas A. and M." *SWHQ*, July 1954, pp. 22–35.

Pool, William C. "Military Aviation in Texas, 1913–1917." *SWHQ*, April 1956, pp. 429–454.

Ragsdale, Kenneth B. *Austin, Cleared for Takeoff*. Austin: University of Texas Press, 2004.

Ragsdale, Kenneth B. *Wings over the Mexican Border: Pioneer Military Aviation in the Big Bend*. Austin: University of Texas Press, 1984.

Revell, Alex. *Fall of Eagles: Airmen of World War One*. South Yorkshire, UK: Pen and Sword Books, 2011.

Rickenbacker, Eddie. *Fighting the Flying Circus*. New York: Frederick A. Stokes, 1919.

Ross, John F. *Enduring Courage*. New York: St. Martin Griffin, 2014.

Rossano, Geoffrey, and Thomas Hildenberg. *Striking the Hornets' Nest: Naval Aviation and the Origin of Strategic Bombing in World War I*. Annapolis, MD: Naval Institute Press.

Sloan, James J. *Wings of Honor: American Airman in World War I*. Atglen, PA: Schiffer Publishing, 1994.

Smith, Douglas V., ed. *One Hundred Years of U. S. Navy Air Power*. Annapolis: Naval Institute Press, 2010.

Sunderman, James F. *Early Air Pioneers*. New York: Franklin Watt, 1961.

Thayer, Lucian H. *America's First Eagles: History of the U. S. Air Service, A.E.F.*, San Jose: James Bender Publishing, 1983.

Tuchman, Barbara. *The Zimmermann Telegram*. New York: Ballantine, 1985.

Vaughan, David K. *Flying for the Air Service*. Bowling Green: Bowling Green State University Popular Press, 1998.

Vaughn, George A. *War Flying in France*. Manhattan, KS: Aerospace Historian Publishing, 1980.

Walker, John Knox. *Over at College: A Texas A&M Campus Kid in the 1930s*. College Station: Texas A&M University Press, 2016.

War Birds: Diary of an Unknown Aviator. New York: George H. Doran Co., 1926.

Wells, H. G. *The War in the Air*. New York: Boni and Liveright, 1917.

White, Lonnie J. "The Call to Arms." *Military History of Texas and the Southwest*, Vol. 17, No. 2, 1982, pp. 1–23.

Winslow, Carroll. *With the French Flying Corps*. New York: Scribner, 1917.

Winter, Lumen, and Glenn Degner. *Minute Epics of Flight*. New York: Grossel and Dunlap, 1933.

Woodall, James R. *12 Texas Aggie War Heroes*. College Station: Texas A&M University Press, 2016.

Wooster, Ralph A. *Texas and Texans in the Great War*. Buffalo Gap, TX: State House Press, 2009.

Wortman, Marc. *Millionaires Unit*. London: Pan Books, 2006.

Newspapers

Air Service Journal, 1917–1918
Austin Statesman, 1917–1919
Bryan Daily Eagle, 1909–1920

Brownsville Herald, 1917–1918
Dallas Morning News, 1916–1920
The Daily Herald (Weatherford, Texas), 1919
El Paso Herald, 1917–1918
Evening Star (Washington, DC), 1913
Fort Worth Star Telegram, 1918
Houston Chronicle, 1914–1918
Houston Post, 1917–1919
Kelly Field Eagle (San Antonio), 1918–1919
Lincoln Star (Nebraska), 1931
San Antonio Express, 1916–1919
Stars and Stripes, 1918
Times (London), 1897, 1914–1919
The Battalion (College Station), 1916–1919
The New York Times, 1916–1919
The Reveille (College Station), 1918
Victoria Advocate, 1988
Wills Point Chronicle, 1919

INDEX